How to Sell Proper

MW01295162

2ⁿᵈ Edition

Understanding Insurance Sales, Tips and Techniques.

Written by Michael Bonilla, CPCU

About the Author.

Believe it or not this section is always the hardest for me to write about. I really don't enjoy talking about myself. I enjoy having people talk about themselves. What do people want to know about an author? Background? Experiences? Belief systems? I enjoy breaking things and putting them back together. What kind of person am I? What kind of person do I want to represent?

Let me tell you a brief story that tells you what kind of person I am. Back in the early 90's I was sketching out my design for a boxcar derby car for boy scouts. This was my first race and I couldn't think of the type of car I wanted to build. To say the least there was zero inspiration. I scribbled out some designs on this piece of paper and eventually after running out of paper went into the den to find more paper. I stopped for a second and glanced over by the window. After staring out of the window for a second (maybe several minutes) I saw my father as he was pulling into the driveway with his 1990 White Dodge diesel, you could hear it for miles.

Then it hit me. What if I used his truck as the design? I re-read the instructions and rules for the derby. The boxcar kit came in a small cardboard box with a block of wood we could use to make our cars. The instructions read as follows:

* Must have 4 wheels
* Must weigh X LBs, no more and no less.
* Must be X inches long by X Inches wide.

So, that being said. Nowhere in the rules/instructions did it specifically say "this boxcar must be a car". So, for the first time in the boxcar derby history. Michael Bonilla entered a truck. To which everyone started laughing. It was a small wooded version of a 1990's Dodge Ram 2500. With a big Pepsi decal on the driver side door. So, we called it the Pepsi truck.

I placed my 'car' on the race line for the first race and hoped for the best. The judges looked at it. It met the weight requirements, the size requirements and had the appropriate amount of wheels. So, we raced and I waited with anticipation for the results. As I was short I couldn't even see the race. All I heard was, "Pepsi truck 1st place." After all 5 races that day I kept hearing those same words over and over again.

After sweeping that year's event. The following year I decided to change it up and make a replica of the Mach 5 Speed Racer Car, in which I came in third place. That next year every 'car' was a truck, besides mine. Don't bend the rules, don't break the rules, test the rules and test the boundaries of the game you are given. Look for loopholes and exploits in the system.

I'm unsure what kind of insight that might have provided. Nevertheless, this book is the longest, most through and probably well thought out I have written to date. I'm an author, a consultant, a former agency owner, an avid golfer, a husband and most importantly someone who enjoys giving back through teaching.

Preface

When a marketing rep comes into your office or someone from the management team and tells you to, 'Sell the value', how often do you find yourself rolling your eyes? As a former agency owner and now a consultant, I often find myself spouting the same slogan. Why? Because, I have done it and done it quite successfully. Whenever a rep came into my office and told me to sell the value of carrier X, I would think that's something an expensive company would say or an overpriced company, because what else could they say?

We've officially entered a hard market cycle in California on the personal lines side, which is strange to even say. The market has tightened up and many carriers are non-renewing or reducing underwriting appetite to not take on a lot of new business in California. This is why I started writing in 2014 and again in 2017, 2018 and 2019. In my estimation our industry is going to see a massive shift over the next 3 or 4 years. A shift from judgement underwriting to block chain and data underwriting. Artificial intelligence has already been underwriting, selling and handling claims for smaller insure-tech companies for the past 4 years. This is a prevalent trend in our industry. But, why?

Why? Because, we have shifted our focus from selling peace of mind to selling a price. Why? Because, we have put more value on talking about premium, payments and price, than having hard conversations about protecting assets and families. We have shifted hard on price, and almost every insurance company has followed suit in their marketing efforts. Almost exclusively every billboard, social media ad and print ad espouses X insurance carrier savings you up to 25-43% on your insurance per year. The conversation has shifted in a way that will cannibalize our industry and wrongfully set expectations for consumers.

A recent study by insurancequotes.com found that around 80% of consumers self-report in blind surveys that consumers shop or are prompted to shop based on price. This study is congruent with most studies down on consumer behaviour.

"If everyone is thinking alike, then somebody isn't thinking." George S. Patton

Contents

"If communication is to change behavior, it must be grounded in the desires and interests of the receivers." Aristotle

Chapter 1: Introduction.

What is our business? What are we in the business of doing? Well, we sell insurance, right? Wrong! Most agents don't realize the kind of business they're in. We are in the peace of mind business. Our business, your business is to sell peace of mind. We are all in the business of providing trust, certainty and ultimately peace of mind. Think differently? Let me ask you something.

What do you buy when you buy insurance? Do you buy 'full-coverage'? Are you just fulfilling a requirement for a lien-holder? What we tend to forget as agents is that overtime the fundamental reason people purchase insurance is so they can buy peace of mind. They are purchasing a simple promise. Heaven forbid your insured should be involved in an accident, you are there to take care of them and help pick up the pieces. Whether that accident was a life-altering accident, maybe they lost their home or were involved in a 5 car pile-up, at the end of the day you sold them a promise.

Have you ever bothered to ask yourself this question? Well, allegedly most people are prompted by price as the reason for shopping for new insurance. But, is that the truth or what people just say as the reason? Let's dig a little bit deeper. People shop on price and all the care about is price, right? Let's explore this concept a bit.

A consumer shows up and wants to save money on their insurance. This is reason why they are speaking with you, right? The problem in the consumer's mind is that they are overpaying and a better deal exists. At least in the mind of the consumer. So, the question I would often ask to a consumer like this is, "How long have you been with Big Captive Insurance?" Normally, the answer is some length of time if the prospect is with a captive insurance company. So, the average length from my experience is around 5 years or so, and potentially much longer. Why does it matter? Well, most all insurance companies take rate increases every single year. Maybe, not massive increases in rate, but at least inflationary increases in rate. Why does it matter? Here's why it matters. The prospect is unhappy with their rate going up and is shopping around the renewal period. But, why this renewal period? What do I mean? Why not the last X amount of years that they go rate increases? Why didn't they shop last year? Why not the last 5 years with Big Captive insurance company? The reason why, the underlying reason why is that the prospect doesn't see the value in paying that price.

Well mike, people don't know what they have until they have to use it. I understand and agree with that. But, often when we start digging into why people ACTUALLY shop for insurance, it's because of a bad experience or lack of experience/expectations met. Maybe, the agent stopped calling on renewals to review insurance coverage, maybe the agent stopped returning phone calls in a timely manner, or possibly there was a snafu in the billing cycle and the insured went into collections, etc. and or etc. Price is merely the cost of value and a surface level concern for most people. Why? Because, we don't buy insurance for the price, we buy insurance and it costs a price. We purchase insurance for peace of mind, financial responsibility laws and many other reasons other than just price.

But Mike, if consumers only care about peace of mind, then why do they switch insurance companies?

People by in large tend to switch insurance companies for three primary reasons.

- They had a bad experience with their Agent.
- They had a bad experience with their insurance company on a claim or billing situation, and the Agent didn't help.
- They had the wrong insurance policy or amount of coverage and found out the hard way.

What is the common thread that links of all these reasons people tend to switch insurance companies? The Agent could have prevented them! The reason I wrote this book is for all the struggling Agents and Brokers. Whether Captive or Independent the fundamental business practices of successful Agents seem to be the same.

What are the three areas of the business every

agent is most concerned about? The rate? The insurance company coming out with a new product? No. Retention, Selling, and Prospecting. In this book we will focus on those three areas of Agency Ownership, because we can control those areas of the business. You'll find a lot of common factors in this book. Focus on what we can control, how we can develop systems and processes to help you succeed.

An Insurance Agency is made up of essentially three core component parts. An Agency can fundamentally be broken down into three aspects; the People, the Processes utilized and the Products offered.

Insurance Agency = Process + Product + People

Every business boils down to three core elements and interdependent parts.

People = How you structure your agency for success.

Product = How you position your product line fo success.

Process = How you prospect, underwrite and sell for success.

What do you picture when you think of an Insurance Agent? What does an Insurance Agent actually do? Believe it or not a lot of seasoned agents can't even answer this question. Why do we even need agents? Most Insurance Agents really are not trained well in understanding actually what an insurance Agent does or can do for a client. Selling insurance is a very small part in what an agent does. An Agent's core activities revolve around Prospecting, Underwriting and Selling Insurance.

An Agent can provide much greater value and service above and beyond those core activities. For instance, home consultations where an agent can actually do some field underwriting. Agents can provide valuable loss prevention tips to consumers, Agents can advise clients on when to self-insure a loss or when to file a claim. Agents can advise clients on their assets exposes to loss and how to mitigate damages during a catastrophe. Agents can educate clients on the financial consequences of loss and how to implement risk management techniques to protect client's assets. Educate clients and customize their insurance coverages to fill gaps.

A lot of agents tell me, "Well, I have great customer service..." Or, "Customers choose me because they know I'll take care of them." Clients want a problem solver more than they want someone to just like them all the time. Don't get me wrong I'm a huge proponent of caring and showing clients we care. Other than customer service, what do you bring to the table in the way of value? If you've read any of my books I constantly ask, "What do you do really well?" Think about that for a second. As your agent I will provide the following and keep these themes at the forefront of the conversation.

- Guidance
- Expertise
- Advising

A lot of people have an idea of what they want, but they don't really know what they need. Right? Everyone wants a cheap price, everyone wants the best company possible and great coverage. This is where proper guidance comes in, this is where being an authority on the subject comes into play. We're licensed, bonded and educated insurance professionals, so start let's acting like it. Advising comes into play on claims, coverage and selecting the appropriate company to fit the risk.

Claims Advising

Sometimes a claim is better off not filed, because it could be self-insured. What happens when you use your insurance too often? You skip go don't collect $200 and go straight to jail. Insurance jail is called the Surplus lines market or in CA the FAIR plan. On average a preferred company uses the 3 strikes rule. If a client uses their insurance 1 or 2 times they are now in California un-eligible for coverage. A client doesn't realize this, they have no clue for the most part. The adjuster won't explain this during the claims process. For the most part the adjuster assesses the claim and settles it. Meanwhile the insured thinks they hit the lottery and there is not risk of using their insurance. Much like talking about consequences of risk, there are consequences of using your insurance too often.

The QERC System

The Q.E.R.C system is a process I put together

that is grounded in the old A.I.D.A selling model. The system is meant to sell concepts and benefits on an insurance policy. So, how does it work? This basic four step process goes as follows:

1. Open with a Question
2. Educate
3. Recommend
4. Close with a Question

The idea is rather simple and relies on a proper conversation about value and needs with an insurance consumer. We use a transitioning question or statement to broach a topic in the first step of the process. We can use a factoid or ask a provocative question to get the process going. For instance, John I noticed that you didn't have Water Back-Up Sewer and Drainage endorsed on your home insurance, can I ask why? This is a simple and easy way to get a conversation going about a benefit and it is an easy way to get the consumer's attention.

The second part of the process is to use the answer as an opportunity to educate the consumer. In the first step we ask a question and in the second we gather data to leverage. This is now a great educational opportunity to pursue. A typical consumer will not have an adequate amount of WBSD on a home policy, either they have nothing or an inadequate amount of around $5000 or so in coverage. This is where we step in an experts and advisors to recommend the proper amount of coverage. The average severity is X and the frequency Y.

The third step in the process is to then make our professional recommendation to the insured. For example, "As your agent I recommend you get BLANK amount of coverage, because of BLANK reason." Give you reason some power by explaining it, not just explaining the coverage. Most agents make the mistake of not asking for the sale, this is part of asking for the sale and getting 'mini-closes' during the sales process.

In the fourth step of the process we now simply 'close' the concept or benefit. For instance, we can then ask the insured, "Is this something you want coverage for?" Now, a lot of agents often ask, "Why even ask for coverage and not just put it on the policy?" The reason why is that we want the insured to think and feel they are the ones making the decision, we are not upselling to upsell or just randomly recommending a lot of coverage. We are having a thoughtful conversation on needs and protection. This will reduce chargebacks and greatly decrease the chance of the insured being uncertain about coverage. Put the onus on the insured to make the decision, this is called selling.

The HAUL System a Selling Framework

What is the typical presentation strategy for insurance agents? Another insurance sales consultant put it best, "Most agents Quote, Copy and Prey." What is the H.A.U.L system and why is it important? The HAUL system is a simple selling framework for multi-line agents to follow as you transition through product lines. Start the conversation with home insurance, transition to auto insurance, cross sell to umbrella insurance and finish by instigating life insurance options.

Learning Phases by Calvin Sun

How do people learn? We go through stages and phases. As you progress in your insurance career at some point you will go through these stages. Reading this book you might find yourself at stage 1 or stage 4. Odds are no matter which stage you find yourself at, you can find something useful in this book. Calvin sun describes the four stages of learning as such:

Stage 1 – Unconscious Incompetence.

Stage 2 – Conscious Incompetence.

Stage 3 – Conscious Competence.

Stage 4 – Unconscious Competence.

Stage 1 – Unconscious Incompetence.

During this stage of learning you don't know what you don't know.

Stage 2 – Conscious Incompetence.

During this stage of learning you know that there are things you don't know. It's a realization of your own ignorance.

Stage 3 – Conscious Competence.

You know what you know and you maybe only put slight thought into an activity.

Stage 4 – Unconscious Competence.

The easiest way to think about this stage of learning is with this question. Do you have to think about how to tie your shows or do you know how to do it without thinking?

The State of the Consumer Insurance Expectations

The truth is that the majority of consumers have no clue how their insurance works. Most consumers don't know what they need either or if what they have is close to what they need. In a recent insurance study by Insurancequotes.com it found that about 50% of personal lines consumers thought they could not shop outside the renewal window. Although, in a similar study 80% of consumers reported shopping due to price as the main factor, only about 20% of insurance consumers are fluid each year.

Trusted Advisor and Personal Risk management

As your agent my job is to protect your stuff. It's really that simple. I'm acting as your personal risk manager. Think of a large company, they have risk management departments and insurance departments, I'm your insurance 'department'. So, in the spirit of being a risk manager let's understand how we must drive the conversation. There are three stages of the conversation and explaining coverage needs.

1. Assets exposed to loss
2. A cause of loss
3. Consequences of loss

Assets Exposed to Loss

If someone needs insurance they have assets, it's as simple as that. Those assets are going to be exposed to potential loss. How do we determine the needs of a consumer? Theoretically, we could just write the same amount of insurance for every customer, right? Why is the customer here? What brought them by today? They have assets to protect! What type of assets do we protect?

- Tangible
- Intangible

What kind of assets does the client have? How long have they had them? What kind of loss experience have they had?

A Cause of Loss

What is a cause of loss? It's a hazard. Fire, flood, earthquake, wind/hail, water damage, theft, vandalism, etc. With each new asset there presents a new set of risks and your risk profile changes.

Consequences of Loss

Consequences of loss are how we sell insurance. At some point in my sales presentation there has to be an 'ah-ha' moment. There has to be some kind of epiphany and realization. What do you to lose?

Two Most Important Rules of Selling Insurance

These are the two rules I lived and died by when I sold insurance. If you take anything from this book let it be these two rules.

> Rule # 1: Never assume the agent before you did their job correctly.
>
> Rule # 2: Don't spend the client's money for them!

Let's examine the first rule. How many declaration pages do you come across with now Water Back-Up Sewer and Drainage coverage? How many policies do you come across with no extended replacement cost coverage? How many policies do you come across with no Med Pay or no rental car coverage? How many policies do you come across with no wedding ring personal article floater? How many policies do you come across with no inflation rider or no personal injury? How many policies do you come across with low deductibles?

Let's examine rule number 2. One of my marketing rep's Scott Matthews, a great human being, once asked me, "Whose job is it to spend the client's money?" It was a startling question from a marketing rep. Why did he ask me this question? Because, the first part of my career I sold insurance on price and not value. For the first part of my career I didn't take the time to understand needs and thoroughly review coverages. When Scott asked me this question I arrived at an inflexion point in my career and started radically altering my process. Let me share an interesting statistic with you.

"57% of customers will take quotes 19% to 53% higher than their current insurance." – Michael Jans (Agencyrevolution.com)

From my experience this number is about right. But, it begs a simple question. Why or in what set of circumstances would a person pay more for their insurance coverage? Because, all people care about is price, right? People will pay more for their insurance, like anything else in life, if you position the product in a way that can justify the value of the price.

"I am the wisest man alive, for I know one thing, and that is that I know nothing." - Plato

Chapter 2: Selling Your Process, Selling Yourself and Selling Your Company/Product

Talent is a process.

Ever wonder what made Tiger Woods the greatest golfer of all time? First and foremost he was dedicated to his craft. But, how did he do it? Tiger Woods from a very young age was taught the correct processes and perfected those processes. There's a reason why to this day he has a gold coach. That's right Tiger Woods has a golf instructor/coach. He also has a personal trainer and a strength trainer and a mental coach.

Ask yourself, what do all of these people help him achieve? They help him stick to a process. They help him perfect those processes. When you are developing your agency stick to process, don't try to reinvent the wheel. When you sell insurance, anything for that matter, it comes down to mastering a process.

What kind of Agency do you want to create/make?

The first step in determining what kind of agency you want to develop/build is proper planning. The best way to do this, for me, was by offering a comprehensive approach to protecting our client's assets. Ask yourself, a few questions:

- What do I want to be known for?
- What kind of business do we want to write?
  - Sub-standard
  - Standard
  - Preferred
  - and or all of the above.
- What kind of clients do you want?
- What kind of insurance do you want to sell?
  - Everything!
  - Commercial Lines
  - Personal Lines
  - Life and Financial
- What does my current company allow me to write?
  - What are my boundaries?
- What is the sweet spot for my company?
  - Where am I most competitive?
- What is an untapped market for my company?

- What's in your wheel house?
- What do you know? Who do you know?
- What is going to build you base of income?
- Do you have a niche?
- Do you belong to some association that will be a good niche to market?

The days of being the do-it-all one stop shop 'insurance guy' are long over. The future of insurance agencies is in having some kind of specialty. Because, a specialty is not a 1-800 number, because a specialty is not a mobile app, because a specialty is not going to be outsourced, easily.

Remember affluent clients or clients who care about protecting their assets or clients who have a unique risk exposure will all value having an expert guide them and take care of them. If you want to be the cheapest auto insurance guy in the valley, more power to you. The point I'm trying to make is that you need to figure out what can make you money and what market is congruent with your practice.

Develop some standards.

Each Agency has to stand for something. Why?

Because, we all eventually have to learn a fundamental truth when it comes to selling insurance. That truth is not every person who walks into your office is going to be a client. My standard was simple, 'I wanted to insure every client as well as I insured my own grandmother.' You can try to be the jack of all trades or you can be a niche agency. All of our standards were focused around achieving a profit bonus. We wanted higher self-insured retention and higher density per household, which in turn would most likely mean rates would be stable and we could achieve our profit bonus.

Some of the standards we developed over time.

- Only took on Clients with EFT or recurring CC.
- Only Proposed 250/500 or higher limits for Auto.
- Presented Umbrella Policies on every sale.
- We did not write limits below 100/300.
- We proposed high deductibles.
- We attempted to meet face to face with 100% of clients.
  - Achieved about 50%.

- We focused on clients with low claims frequency and or low severity.
- Never sell an auto without Rental/Med Pay

But Mike, Isn't insurance a commodity and people only care about rate?

No. People focus on price as a factor, but it is not the determining factor. Have you ever heard a client say, "I don't think this is in my budget." Or give you some clearly bogus price objection. Remember people buy things outside of their budget all the time, that's why we all have credit cards. If you want to think insurance is all about the rate then you just haven't learned how to sell insurance based on value.

Selling You. Selling Your Product/Process/Service. Selling your company.

I'm a strong believer that people tend to think in patterns, specifically in threes. Our focus was protecting middle class families by offering the highest quality auto, home and umbrella protection on the market. Stick to presenting things in threes.

Selling You – Selling you is simple. What do

you offer? Why should someone sign up with your agency/brokerage?   One of my favorite questions to ask agents is, "Why should a client sign up with you and not the guy down the street? Can you answer that question?

Selling Your Product/Process/Service – This is your unique value proposition. Our process was simple, we first educated our clients on their insurance needs (assets exposed to loss and consequences), made a recommendation to protect those assets and finally customized to match the coverage for each client's specific situation as needed (sometimes they didn't want certain types of coverage or wanted more coverage.)

My shtick went something like this, "I just have a few quick question and then I'll hand it back over to you to see if you have any concerns or questions. Other than that I'll take the info I have and prepare a proposal for you and hopefully we can help you out. Here's my approach and I take my approach in a lot of detail. You've got a lot going on in your life and dealing with insurance is probably on the bottom of your favorite things to do list. So, I'll do all the heavy lifting. And as we get to the end of the process and it really doesn't take that long... What I think you'll find is that you'll feel a lot more comfortable with your insurance and making sure that your protected. In a nutshell what we do is we spend the time to educate you about your risk and your needs, make a professional recommendation around that conversation and then we fit the coverage to meet your specific budget."

Selling Your Company – Selling your company is fluid. It can be challenging at times as you have no control on public perception of that company. Your company is going to change and the insurance company you represent might change drastically over time.

Developing Your Personal Brand.

It's funny we can make as much money as a Lawyer or a Doctor but forgo years of extra education. We tend to forget sometimes that insurance, although at the lower end of the financial services industry, is still in the financial services industry. So, develop your brand accordingly.

Branding is simply what helps a consumer differentiate your product from the next. What does your Agent represent? What do people think of when they think of the BLANK Insurance Agency? What kind of customers do you want to attract? Is your Agency Credible? Is this agent trustworthy? If I didn't sign up with this agent, would I still refer people to them?

The biggest part of branding is understanding what you do and who you serve. Some Insurance Agents try to sell insurance to anyone for any line of insurance they have available under their license. Some Agents like myself chose to have narrow markets and a focused strategy (which we will explore later on in the book). At first I was trying to sell insurance to anyone that fogged a mirror, let me tell you from firsthand experience that is a terrible idea.

How an Agent speaks about their brand usually can be filtered down into two telling statements:

- Transactional Agent, "I sell Auto, Home, Life and Business Insurance."

- Trusted Advisor, "I protect families by educating and implanting risk management strategies with Auto, Home, Life... etc.

Developing a Business Level Strategy

There are two types of strategies to market your insurance practice and help you sell insurance.

1. Cost leadership, "We sell the cheapest insurance."
2. Differentiation, "We do things differently process oriented."

Selling based on price is becoming less and less of an option these days, why? Insurance companies are tightening up underwriting standards for the agency distribution channel and lowering commissions. Which means it's more important than ever to maximize every single sale. The reason for that is because online or direct companies are cutting out brokers and agents all together. Develop a strategy you are comfortable with and that fits the type of clients you are looking to serve.

"The value of an idea lies in the using of it." Thomas A. Edison

Chapter 3: Staffing an Agency

Staffing is one of the hardest parts of developing a successful practice. But, if you speak to the truly successful Agents/Brokers, it really is the fastest way to prosperity. Selling insurance doesn't happen in a vacuum, you'll need help eventually and as soon as possible.

But Mike, Why should I staff my Agency?

Great question! Ask yourself, are you happy working 80 hours a week? Are you happy cold calling? Are you looking to run a business or have your business run your life? A few considerations:

1. To scale your business.
2. To make your life easier.
3. So you can work smarter not harder.
4. Increases your valuation.
5. Demand/Capacity, remember there is only so much you can accomplish by yourself.

But Mike, If I want to grow how should I staff my Agency?

That's a good question. The answer is there is

no one size fits all magic pill for agency growth. I know Agents who run call centers out of their office in the attempt to 'grow' producers. I met with an aggregator type agency in Texas two weeks ago that did just that. What I did was start small with Interns to help with minor non-insurance related activities. As we grew we hired producers and a CSR.

Remember, producers are human beings and they will only generate so much new business on their own before they blow through their centers of influence, just like you did as a new agent. We hired telemarketers to dial and smile and we hired online marketers. Did we get a lot of success with telemarketing? Not really.

As a rule of thumb I did at least 30 minutes of telemarketing affluent areas per day to stay sharp and sometimes get high quality leads.

I wish there was a simple plug and play formula that worked for every single agency, there isn't. No one single approach is vastly superior to another. You really just have to experiment and see what fits for your agency.

What I recommend is talking to your colleagues and finding your own path to success. Success leaves clues and people who have done it will share with you how they became successful. I've tried all sorts of compensation schedules and overrides for my agency, it's a work in progress.

But Mike, Does Telemarketing still work?

Yes... No... Maybe. The problem with telemarketing is that most people are not home during the daytime when your business is open. So, you can have later hours to reach people as they get home from work. Because, I know the first thing I want to do when I walk in the door is talk to an insurance telemarketer. It's costly from a training prospective and costly from a compliance perspective to avoid any TCPA complaints.

Also, the people who you generally hire for these roles are not born sales people or have any kind of basic phone handling skills. It's not easy to keep people either as the turn over for telemarketing is 90% in the first 3 months or so.

But Mike, how should we staff out an Agency?

The key question to ask is what job do you want to stop doing? What job do you currently have that you would no longer like to do so you can free up time selling insurance or working on marketing. An employee can be described with a simple goal, to make their managers life easier.

But Mike, How do I pay my staff?

Variable compensation based on incentives tends to be an effective route. Remember people fundamentally operate in the work environment under a simple premise. People work and operate with their own self-interest in mind. So, why not design a compensation package around incentives. Why is it that commission only sales people tend to fail? Because, they are not agents and require support. So keep that in mind.

As an Agent when you started, did you have a stream of income to help you along the way or did you start from scratch? There is a right balance for each staff member. Put some thought into and make sure to build incentives. You can build incentives around growth or around retention or around quality of business written. Don't forget to be creative.

But Mike, hiring people is difficult... do I have to?

No. But, do you want your business to run you or do you want to run your business? Do you want your life to be easier or harder? What do you want to the evolution of your business to look like? Do you want to play defense or offense? In the insurance industry there is no such thing as sitting on the side lines, either you are growing or shrinking.

"We often miss opportunity because it's dressed in overalls and looks like work" — **Thomas A. Edison**

Chapter 4: Prospecting, Marketing & Consumer insights

What is marketing? The best answer I have ever heard came from an overpaid consultant who was giving a speech at my university. He said, 'Marketing is simply a search for the truth.' The number one challenge facing agents is having enough qualified prospects to speak with.

Prospecting

Have you heard the old selling saying, "Prospecting is about talking to enough people and consistently saying the right things."

The easiest <u>Prospecting</u> technique I've ever learned. Just ask these four questions.

1. What do you do for a living/fun?
2. How long have you been doing that for?
3. What do you like about it?
4. How did you get into that? (Job or Activity)
5. What do you do really well?

Worry no longer! The truth is that most people are not interesting, because they don't know how to be interesting. Most people don't live exciting lives or know how to tell captivating tales of adventure and mystery. If you don't know how to be interesting learn first to become interested in other people. More specifically in what people care about the most. What is everyone's favorite subject? Themselves. Until they have kids. So, ask questions about the person.

Should I do Business over the in-person/phone/email?

Nobody wants to meet in person anymore!!!! You're right. I don't meet with my doctor in person, I don't meet with my accountant in person, I don't meet with my attorney in person, I don't meet with my professors in person, I don't meet with my wife in person... People spend time with things and people they care about. If something is important enough to you, you tend to make it a priority. Some people don't want to meet in person, it's true. But, did you ask? Ninety-nine percent of the time the agent doesn't ask for an in-person meeting and assumes the client wants to do business over the phone. Don't just assume, ask.

There are many different schools of thought on this. Most people like to do business thru the modality they choose and not the modality you chose for them in your mind. Some people want to buy insurance via email and E-signatures. Some people want to use WebMD, some people want to use TurboTax and some people want to use lawyers in a box. Some people want to buy insurance thru a mobile app. Some people like to look around online and then talk to an actual person. Some people want to talk to an expert in person.

JD Power runs a study each year for Insurance Consumer shopping habits. The study found in 2016 that 74% of consumers use insurer websites or aggregators for obtaining quotes and researching information. But, only 25% actually purchase their policy online. The point I'm trying to make is, whatever is congruent for you, do it. What doesn't work with your flow, simply discard it.

Add these questions to your process. When would be a good time to come by the office? Or would you rather meet at your home or business? Mind-blowing I know, the 1950's called and want their qualifying questions back. Would you be able to meet on Tuesday at 6 or Thursday at 6? Which time would work better for you?

A broken clock is right twice a day.

Sometimes when prospecting you just hit the right person at the right time, "I've been meaning to talk to somebody about my insurance." Guess what? I'm your huckleberry. Even if you're bad at prospecting somebody out there is always looking for insurance.

Selling over the Phone vs In Person?

If you choose to sell over the phone you can achieve a much higher contact rate. You can contact more people more often. The main advantage to meeting in person is that you closing rate dramatically increases. It increases because you can illustrate coverages for purposes of upselling. You can actually see buying signal. It's a lot harder to say no in person rather than over the phone. If someone actually shows up in person it shows they care or have concerns they want a professional to address.

How do I get them into the office?

Depends on the client. For most clients it's tough for scheduling purposes. But, just ask. Insurance is by in-large still a relationship business. If you are in the price gouging and coverage stripping business then good luck competing with online insurance companies who have billion dollar marketing budgets.

For example,

Agent: Okay I have most of your info that we need to start looking at some options. Now what's a good time of day to meet morning, afternoon or evening?

Prospect: Can't you explain this over the phone? Or can't you just give me a number?

Agent: I most certainly can. But as a rule for my

Agency, I take protecting your assets very seriously and if you have 5 or 10 minutes I would like to sit down with you and your wife (slight pause) and explain how this policy works to protect your assets.

Agent: Bob, I sure can. And I'm sure a lot of Agents will just throw out numbers to try and earn your business. What I've found in my practice is that when it comes to protecting everything you care most about in this world (slight pause) your family... your assets... it's usually better to take 5 or 10 minutes and sit down to evaluate your current protection. (Shut Up and wait for an answer)

Usually at this point you get one of two responses.

Prospect: Okay.

Or

Prospect: I'd rather just do this over the phone.

Even if you don't meet in person at least you

made an attempt to meet in person. It's better to try and not succeed than never try at all.

What Percentage of Customers Move Companies Each Year?

From industry research we know the insurance market is about 20% fluid. Which means the average retention for an insurance company is around 80%. Why is this important? This shows that at least 30% of consumers shop every year. How do we know this? Because, statistically speaking out of that 20% of consumers that is fluid, it's not likely that represents 100% of consumers who shopped.

What Percentage of Customers Shop Each Year?

There's not an actual definite answer to this question. But, latest research from insurance quotes shows 8% of people shop for insurance multiple times per year, 25% Once a year, 27% Every Few Years and 39% never.

Who are the insurance shoppers?

There are 7 types of insurance shoppers, Price Shoppers, Bargain Shoppers, Convenience Shoppers, Relationship Shoppers, Coverage Smart Shoppers and Vengeance Shoppers. These are categories in my firm we put each client into. Once we knew who we were dealing with it was easier to tailor make our presentation to suit their needs or know whether or not to refer them to another firm.

Price Shoppers – usually a customer in the sub-standard market, higher claims frequency, usually does not understand how insurance works, shops frequently, lower deductibles, etc.

Bargain Shoppers – you'll find these shoppers in any market. Typically they have lower claims frequency but are looking to save money for equal or better coverage.

Convenience Shoppers – Some consumers understand the value of insurance but have policies that are scattered all over the place. They might have so many polices that they do not know what they have exactly. They are looking to simplify and will pay more for it. Other convenience shoppers just want to know as their agent you will 'take care of them'. As their agent they want you to make their life easier.

Relationship Shoppers – These shoppers shop because of an existing relationship.

Coverage Smart Shoppers – Coverage shoppers have assets or aspire to one day have assets and want protection. They want certainty that a claim if filed will be paid and that they are paying for the protection. They understand the value of insurance and appreciate education.

Vengeance Shoppers – These shoppers had a bad experience with a claim, a bad experience with billing or the insurance company and or a bad experience with their agent. Spite is a great motivator. I do things all the time that people tell me I can't do or goals I can't achieve.

New Entries – Newly divorced spouses who never handled insurance or new first time home buyers and or youthful drivers getting of their parents insurance.

But Mike, how do I figure out which shopper I'm dealing with?

It's a lot easier said than done and a lot of shoppers tend to have overlapping areas of concerns or reasons for shopping. Remember, not all of these types are mutually exclusive.

Identifying a Price Shopper

Agent: How can we help?

Prospect: "I want/need to pay less for insurance."

Agent: Okay, besides price what do you care about?

Prospect: "I just want the cheapest insurance possible."

Identifying Bargain Shoppers

Agent: How can we help?

Prospect: "I (think or feel) that I'm paying too much for insurance."

Prospect: "We've been reviewing our budget and think we are looking for areas to save."

Agent: Great. The fastest way to save money with insurance is by looking at slightly higher deductibles. How about we bump up your collision from $500 to $1000?

Identifying Convenience Shoppers

Agent: How can we help?

Prospect: I've got a lot of insurance and would like to see what's out there.

Agent: Well, let me ask you something Bob, if I could find a way to bundle all of your policies, would that be something you would consider paying a little more for that?

Prospect: Yes, but obviously it depends on how much more.

Identifying Relationship Shoppers

These are friends, family or Co-workers. Maybe a neighbor. Someone who feels that they have somewhat of an obligation to shop based on knowing the Agent. The shoppers are also unhappy with their current agent or level of service provided by that agent.

Identifying Coverage Shoppers

Agent: What brings you by today?

Prospect: I'm not sure I have the proper amount of coverage.

Agent: Okay, why do you feel that way? (Or better yet) When was the last time your Agent reviewed your coverage?

Prospect: When I first signed up 10 years ago.

What do all of these consumers have in common?

They are looking for you to solve a problem. The price consumer wants you to provide a cheaper price, the bargain shopper a better value, the convenience shopper to make their life easier, the relationship shopper has an obligation to shop based on an existing relationship and the vengeance shopper just wants you to move.

Insurance Marketing 101

I'm only going to briefly touch base on marketing as a set aside an entire supplemental book for it called, "How to market modern insurance agencies."

How many should I have?

There is no arbitrary right number of marketing activities. The idea is to find activities that are congruent with your selling style and your life style. For a base number of marketing activities you should have around 3 to 5 to start with and build off of.

How long should I give the system?

Marketing is more of an art form than a science. Why? Because, people are different. As wildly controversial and insightful that last statement was, take the time to know you audience. Don't set yourself up for failure. Most agents want instant results and unless you are working internet leads, plan on giving the activity some time to produce. Most agents invest in a system for a month and then give up if it doesn't produce. Why give up so quickly? This business is cyclical and maybe that month is a bad month to hit people. As a rule of thumb I gave every marketing campaign or activity a solid year to maturate.

Niche Marketing

Again with Niche Marketing it comes back to what your company can write and what is within your wheelhouse. Here are a few ideas of Niche Marketing:

1. **Previous Loss History Homes**: Homes with loss history are hard to write and lead companies usually offer a discount as Agents for the most part stay away.

2.   **Dogs in the Home or Animals**: Most insurance companies stray away from very common dog breeds and can open markets for you. Properties with horses are typically hard to place or Farm Animals.

3.   **HomeWork**: Clients who have home based businesses often need specialized coverage on their Ho3.

4.   **RideShare**: Rideshare endorsements are offered by only a handful of companies. If you happen to represent one think about it as an open market.

5.   **HomeShare:** AirBnB and other Home-Sharing companies are becoming extremely popular and are generally hard to place risk.

6.   **Targeted Risk Clients:** Ever read the liability exclusions based on profession or famous people? These are people who are targets for liability risk and hard to place.

But Mike, in the age of Internet insurance companies how do I market?

What I found particularly effective was a combination of networking and digital marketing based on our niche. See below for ideas. You cannot out market Compare.com or the direct writing insurance carriers.

Cold Calling

Cold calling can be a great way to raise your blood pressure. But, for insurance marketing it can be somewhat inconsistent. I take a lot of pride in my cold calling abilities. I once taught a 16 year old with no insurance knowledge to get leads. The problem is that no matter how good of a cold caller you are is that the burn out rate is incredibly high. Cold calling works if you have a good script. Cold calling works if you use an automated dialer. Cold calling works if you play the numbers and call at the right time.

Cold Calling Script

Sample Script. This is modeled after and almost the exact transcript from a **40 minute cold call** I had with a prospect. During the call he actually took the time to look up his current insurance policies online and review them via phone so I could run comparisons. This was a highly educated client with lots of assets.

Agent: "Hi is BLANK Home?"

Prospect: "Yeah. What'd you want?"

Agent: 'Hi my name is BLANK with BLANK Agency. How you doing today?" (Please alter the language I grew up raided by Italians from the Bronx)

Prospect: "I'm good."

Agent: "The reason for the call today is INSERT REASON. Think you have thirty seconds to talk?" (Going for a Yes response)

Agent: "The reason for the call today is INSERT REASON. Is this a bad time to talk?" (Going for a No response)

Agent: "The reason for the call today is INSERT REASON. Think you can give me a couple minutes talk?" (Going for a Yes response)

Prospect: Yes, no or maybe. (Gotta hit them at the right time.)

Agent: Can I ask you one question. Who are you currently insured with?

From this point just go into your normal qualifying workflow. Ask the important questions for rating and lock-down a commitment for a follow-up appointment.

Agent: John, I just want to thank you for spending the time to see if we could help you out today. Now, as I take this info and go put some options together for you, what kind of questions did you have for me?

Agent: (Handle outstanding questions or concerns) Would you rather come by the office or have me run by the house really quick to drop off the proposals? When would be a good time to touch base Tuesday at 6 or Thursday at 6?

Internet Leads

Current Environment: 'Exclusive Internet Leads' are sold sometimes to 3 or 4 Agents and then the data is resold to other lead companies. About 5% of leads are valid if you buy generic leads.

Mistakes Agents Make: Not working leads as soon as they come in and not returning leads when they are not valid leads. Also, not having a good follow up and drip system.

What I've found to work: Firstly, you need a system in place to work the leads. An automated follow up system that connects your phone to the lead or a dialing system. Also, some lead systems connect with your CRM so you can call the prospect with a quote almost in real time.

Remember internet leads is all about the sheer volume and ordering enough to filter out the bad leads. Also, the more specific lead you purchase the less competition you have to deal with.

For instance, for internet leads we had massive success with two lines of business. We had great success with High Risk Home Insurance and Specialty products. People with claims? Let me ask you something. As an underwriter is a homeowner whose house burned down a bad risk? Yes, of course? Really, why? The home was rebuilt and paid for by the last company. It's a brand new home you are insuring, new pipe, new sprinkler system, new heating and air, new roof. Just one bad day. Could happen to anyone.

Sales Process: Internet Leads

Working internet leads is a vastly different process than your typical referral process. To be effective Internet leads need to be worked immediately, a system has to be set up to automate the follow up and contact process. If the leads are invalid, the leads need to be returned immediately for lead credit. If the prospect answers, but does not follow up they need to be re-marketed via drip campaigns and squeeze pages. If the lead is within driving distance you should ask for an in-person appointment.

"Knowledge alone does not produce wisdom." –
Daisaku Ikeda

Chapter 5: Retention

Remember, people tend to switch insurance companies for three primary reasons:

- They had a bad experience with their Agent.
- They had a bad experience with their insurance company on a claim or billing situation, and the Agent didn't help.
- They had the wrong insurance policy or amount of coverage and found out the hard way.

But Mike, Don't people switch because their rate went up?

Yes, some people do. Most people that do this do so because their Agent didn't give them a heads up before the letter got sent out from the insurance company or the Agent didn't do an annual review or the Agent didn't try to find a solution. Remember, we are notified of renewal rates 90 days prior to the renewal.

How much of the Market is Fluid?

It's estimated that about 20 percent of the

insurance market is fluid, more or less. That means at least 20 percent of your customers will be shopping you each year. Princeton funded an insurance survey that I found rather interesting. The survey reported that 66% of customers shopped every few years or never over a 13 year period. The study also found that 7% of consumers shopped multiple times per year and about 27% consumers shopped once a year.

Why is retention so important?

Ask yourself, what do you think a customer acquisition cost is for an insurance customer? This is the reason that acquisition costs are so high. Because, for the most part this is still primarily a relationship business. I'd estimate about for every $300 to $400 you invest in non-networking based marketing you can expect a single customer. If the average home premium is $1000 and the average commission rate is $150, then you can expect that it takes roughly two years to break even on your marketing investment. So, if you lose the client in the first year your return on equity will be negative 50% for all of your marketing. Does it make sense to walk customers in the front door of the business only to lose those same customers out of the backdoor?

More on Retention

The average captive/independent insurance agency has about an 85% retention ratio. Retention has a lot to do with the value the customer perceives relative to their actual budget. Action is dictated by perception. Sometimes customers will leave because of a billing issue or something out of your control. It happens.

For Instance, if the rates go up and customer sees no correlation to value there is a high probability that they shop around for a better value. When a customer shops it's most likely because they received a renewal notice and you didn't bother to call. Agents/Brokers are usually given 90 day notices of a renewal increase. Use that information, don't run from it.

But Mike, how can I hedge my bets?

The simplest way is density per household for PIF. The more policies and endorsements someone has the less likely they are to shop out of sheer laziness. Before sold our business I believe if you include life insurance our average PIF per household was around 4.

Here is a breakdown of the numbers:

1. For a Monoline Auto or Home Policy the average lifespan is 12 month to 14 months.
2. For an Auto and Home Policy the average life span is 18 months to 24 months.
3. For a household with 3 or more polices the average life span is 3 to 5 years.

But Mike, What can I do besides just writing more policies to add value?

Here are some ideas to increase retention based on value:

- Customer Appreciation BBQ/Cook Outs
- Thank you cards/calls
- Claims Follow Up
- Annual Insurance Review
- Birthday and Holiday Cards
- Open Houses

A big opportunity as an independent agent for me was the fact that the captive insurance agent wouldn't pick up the phone when a client called. Out of fear of a tough conversation or who knows what. I can't tell you how many customers we picked up who said, "My agent never calls me."

Remember people like to be cared about, the simplest way to do that is by showing them you care. A great opportunity to add some value and help prevent shopping is to sit down with your customer and review their needs on a yearly basis.

Don't force them to meet once a year, just ask. How often would you like to sit down and evaluate make sure we keep everything current? Part of your qualifying process can be asking this question before you close the sale. As a rule of thumb when it comes to protecting your family, we like to sit down on an ongoing basis to re-evaluate your insurance protection. How often would you like to meet? (Because everyone is different.) Once a year? Twice a year?

Another huge transition we used was this when a prospect had not reviewed their insurance in 5 or 10 years. I'd always be able to tell by looking at the reconstruction cost for a home. "John, when was the last time your agent sat down to review your insurance and make sure it's still current?"

And normally if they were shopping the answer was almost certainly, "When the policy was first written." And usually my response was something to the extent of, "John would it be fair to say that a lot in your life over the past X amount of years has changed?" Or, "Has anything changed in your life in the past X amount of years?" The answer is obvious and would usually result in my ability to compare apples to oranges and sell the correct amount of insurance.

One of the best ways to keep customers is maintaining that face to face trusted advisor role. As a rule of thumb we sat down at least once a year with each of our clients to make sure their assets were not exposed. Life happens and people change. They buy new cards, they change jobs, they buy motorcycles, etc. Sometimes they forget to mention it to you.

Think of it this way, if they are sitting down with you, they are most likely not going to be sitting down with someone else.

Claims follow-up

As Insurance Agents we sell a promise. It's up to the insurance company to get the insured back to normal. Although we just sell the promise, the Agent can play a big role in how the promise is executed.

I'm not asking you as an Agent to do the work for the insurance company. Even if your insurance company might be asking, softly.

An Agent has the power of following up throughout the process with the Adjuster and with the insured will add a tremendous amount of value to the process from the insured perspective. One of the key indicators for an insured's level of claims satisfaction is the Agent getting involved as the advocate for the insured. Trust me I did a brief stint as a claims adjuster. Having the agent hold the claims department accountable is paramount to the outcome. Most customers I would speak with who didn't have the agent at least call, would often ask, "What am I paying that guy for?"

Thank you calls

People crave appreciation and validation. Remind clients that you care about protecting them not just collecting those premium payments and they tend to stick around.

Welcome Packets

There's something about handing someone something tangible that really adds a lot of value. Especially when we sell an intangible promise. Simply put together a nice welcome packet packed with some business cards, a policy, some magnets, etc.

Birthday Cards

Birthday calls are important to maintain a proper relationship with clients in any business climate. Think about how many people contact you on your birthday.

Holiday cards

Holiday cards can be a fun way to show your clients that you care. Pick one obscure holiday each year to send a card out. National hamburger day, or whatever.

"In all chaos there is a cosmos, in all disorder a secret order." Carl Jung

Chapter 6: The Science of Selling

A lot of selling boils down to having a consistent process, playing the odds and following up. Because, just like Bob Burg said, "All things being equal people tend to do business with those they like, trust and know." I don't believe in luck, I believe in odds. So how do we do that? Here are a few ways...

How do we increase your odds of making a sale?

- Face to Face Appointments yield higher results than over the phone/email.
- Get the client's Dec Page, a big part of selling property and casualty sales (when price is not the focus) is picking apart a poorly designed policy or an out of date policy.
- Do not make a habit of emailing quotes. It's a lot easier to say no through an email than in person.
- Dress for the client.
- Buying Insurance is an exclusive process as some companies reject risk and policies cannot be transferred.
- Be agreeable not confrontational.

- Learn to care but not over-care.
- The more you can evoke emotion in your presentation and show someone you care the higher likelihood they will do business with you.
- Ask open-ended questions to uncover personal experiences of the client.
- Customize your insurance proposal to suit the client's specific needs.
- Present every appropriate product at the first meeting and don't just try to win pieces of business.
- Present premium on a monthly basis not yearly. Remember smaller numbers when it comes to expense and larger numbers when it comes to coverage. When you purchase sugar at the grocery store do you look for the cheapest price or the lowest price per unit?
- Understand the relationship of the current advisor/agent.
- Lead with value and not price, price is merely the cost of value.
- Maximize the benefit while minimizing the cost. If you don't 'beat' the price swing for the

fences. Sometimes it's better to compare apples to oranges if you know they have rotten apples. If a prospect has 15/30 and needs 250/500, quote what they need to protect their assets.

Foot-in-the-door (FITD) **technique** is a compliance tactic that involves getting a person to agree to a large request by first setting them up by having that person agree to a modest request.

Using the foot in the door technique is subtly done throughout the process as you get the prospect engaged in your presentation. Remember a sale is a reciprocal exchange of ideas. You are not forcing someone to think like you, you are opening their mind to new ways of thinking.

But Mike, why should I present in person and not through email?

In 1971, Albert Mehrabian published a book called Silent Messages, *in which he discussed his research on non-verbal communication. He concluded that prospects based their assessments of credibility on factors other than the words the salesperson spoke:*

1. **55 percent** *to the speaker's* **body language**.
2. **38 percent** *to the* **tone** *and music of their voice.*
3. **7 percent** *to the salesperson's* **actual words.**

When selling in person you have a captive audience. When selling in person you can illustrate and use a white board or pad of paper.

Over the phone you can reach a lot of people quickly with no geographical boundaries. But, the major trade-off is the loss of body language. The loss of actually seeing the person. There is no more showmanship left in this industry. Insurance doesn't have to be a dull conversation. It can be interesting and emotional.

Think about it this way. Have you ever read a text message and inferred the person's tone of voice from reading it? I'd imagine this has been the unintentional torpedo of many relationships.

Expert hostage negotiator and ex-FBI Chris Voss has a simple negotiation lesson he likes to espouse, "Never be so sure of what you want that you are wouldn't be willing to take something better." This is the idea that you want to plant in the consumer's mind. This is the seed we need to plant to get them to up-sell and cross-sell. This is the seed we need to plant to get them to pay more for insurance, because it would be in their best interest.

Supernormal stimuli is a rather simple concept. A scientist ran a study on eggs and birds. The study found that over-exaggerated features on eggs drives the behavior of birds. For instance, the scientist created fake over-sized bird eggs and presented them to a bird that was currently sitting on her own real eggs. The bird made the choice to actually sit on the fake eggs over her own real eggs. This study basically reiterates the old model of bigger is better.

Okay, so why is any of this important to me? Well, if you present a better product with more coverage, the majority of people in front of you will probably take you up on it. Assuming the price isn't drastically higher. This is why product comparison is crucial for success in selling insurance.

Give and Take

If an insurance sale is a search for the truth we need to follow the rule of reciprocity. The rule of reciprocity makes the insurance buying process a collaborative effort not a confrontational one. Remember, you don't make money until the person signs on the dotted line. We are salespeople first and educators second, because we don't get paid to just educate. This is the key to reciprocity. I'm going to take the time to sit down and analyze your needs and educate you about those needs. In return there is an implicit social arrangement that you will at least hear out my offer. You ask questions to evoke emotions during the process and client has questions that you answer to provide certainty.

The reason why we focused so much on processes in this book is because each sale is more or less always going to be the same. It has an opening and a closing and somewhere in between you talk about stuff important to the prospect. Why are people great salespeople? Because, they have developed a coherent repeatable process for selling.

Think people vs Feel people

Active listening is somewhat of a lost art form in modern selling. Most sales people tend to ask a question and have the prospect rush through the answer or even answer themselves without even letting the prospect think about the question.

Let the prospect answer and let them think! How that person answers will tell you a lot about how to ask your next question. Or if they are giving off buying signals and you can close them earlier than you thought. Selling is a fluid situation, it changes. For instance, people tend to give you clues as to their thought process. For instance, some people respond emotionally with feelings. I really feel that blah, blah, blah... Or they respond more analytically, I think... blah... blah.

There is nothing more frustrating than talking to a salesperson who is rushing you through the process and while you are answering a question you can tell all they are thinking about is what they are going to say next as opposed to digesting your thoughts. If you have sold to scientist or engineers then you can think fairly easily of this distinction.

Preheat the oven before you stick the Turkey in...

Remember, the client doesn't want an instant solution. First we gotta listen. Then we gotta ask questions and do some more listening. After getting an answer we ask follow up questions. New Agents tend to get so eager to write business they tend to skip all that and just start slinging solutions. It was a conclusion we arrived at together after looking at their assets and looking at the size of liability claims that go to court. How hard is it to sell a $150 umbrella policy?

Don't answer your own questions!

No matter how awkward the conversation gets, if you ask a question wait for an answer. Don't rush the person into answering or answer for them. Your job is to be inquisitive and design solutions. This comes back to that old phrase telling is not selling. If it's a tough question wait for an answer.

Telling vs Selling

When presenting concepts it's important to do so

in the form of a question. Why? Because, that is how you sell. Merely explaining concepts isn't enough. Well how do we do that? Easy!

I'm struggling to Up-Sell Med Pay.

How do you sell Med Pay? Most new agents try explaining the coverage and talking about claims severity. Here is a side by side example.

Telling: You only have $5000 in Med Pay.

Selling: I noticed you only have $5000 in Med Pay, can I ask why?

Telling: Med Pay is blah, blah, blah.

Selling: How much do you think it would cost to get an ambulance ride? Do you think your health insurance coverage would pay for it?

Telling: You should get Med Pay.

Selling: Is that something you want coverage for?

Justify the Price, Sell the Value.

Our job as salespeople is to justify the price of what we're selling. I had a client come into my office one time and get a quote. The quote was significantly lower in premium and higher in coverage. So, naturally I thought this was a slam dunk prospect. The prospect thanked me for my time after I hastily ran through my sales presentation. The prospect didn't end up signing up with us. Why do you think that happened? I asked myself this question many times over, as it was on its face a far superior offer. Maybe the client didn't like me, maybe they just wanted something to hand their agent to keep them honest or maybe, just maybe I got overconfident and lazily slapped together a sales presentation that didn't justify the value.

"Don't become a mere recorder of facts, but try to penetrate the mystery of their origin." - Ivan Pavlov

Chapter 7: Selling Insurance as a Process

What do you sell when you sell insurance? You sell a promise and you sell peace of mind. When selling insurance think of it like a search for the truth. What is that truth? Well it's different for every prospect. But, the truth is most people are grossly under-insured. Not every prospect needs umbrella insurance. But, I'd rather have one and not need it than need it and not have one.

Explain the coverage, product comparison.

When was the last time someone actually sat down and explained to you how your coverage actually works? Maybe 10 years ago or never. This is the essence or foundation of our job as agents and if you don't spend the time to do this, what real value can you add? Explain the coverage line by line, why? Because, if the person is open to learning you can easily add value. Why? Because, not everyone you meet is going to be an insurance expert.

Opening Questions

Your opening questions are extremely important because it sets expectations for the entire presentation. This is where you get the prospect engaged and show them that you care. *Remember caring is infectious we all want to have people around us that care about us. So gear your initial questions as open ended.*

Here are a couple of opening questions:

- Before we get started tell me, what kind of questions or concerns do you have about your current insurance?
- How can I help?
- What brings you by today?

Why these questions? The first part of our job isn't to educate, it's to notice and investigate things. Why is your proposal like this? Why are you shopping? What are you looking for in your insurance relationship? What do you expect of an agent? How fast do you want to get a policy in place?

Qualifying Questions

Why do we need qualifying questions? It's like John Madden said, "Don't pull your hose out until you know where the fire is."

- Besides price, what do you care about?
  - o Wait for an answer...
- **Common Answer:** Well, I'd like my Agent to call me once in a while. (Communication is important or lacking currently)
- **Common Answer:** Well, I don't know if I have the right amount of coverage or enough insurance. (No Certainty)
- **Common Answer**: I want to be with a large company. (Financial Certainty)
- **Common Answer:** I recently had a bad experience with billing. (Insurance company accidently sent client into collections or cancelled policy.)

These are all concerns you have to uncover by asking open ended questions and then following up with some specific follow up questions to guide the client through the process.

Most of the time all you have to do is sit back and listen and the prospect will tell you what they are truly concerned about.

- How do you feel about your current insurance protection?
- What else besides blank are you concerned about?
- Do you feel you have enough insurance?
- How do you feel about Sewer Back Up Coverage?
- How do you feel about insuring your wife's wedding ring? I noticed that you didn't have BLANK on your policy, can I ask why?
- It does me no good to sell you something that does you no good.
- There is no such thing as a good deal for a bad policy.
- Would you consider paying slightly more for your insurance if I could put all your policies in one spot? Or get you better coverage?
- Besides price, what's important to you?
- How much does an ambulance ride cost? Will your health insurance cover it?
- How much does a retainer on a good attorney cost?
- What do you like about your current plan?

- What are you looking to do?

What does your qualifying process look like?

Asking open ended questions is the best way to qualify a client. It helps them think about insurance in a different way than they are used to. It helps a prospect be exposed to a different way of buying insurance. Most people expect a boring process where at the end you will spew out some numbers. Be different. As an agent, selling really just involves knowing what to ask, how to ask and when to ask a probing question.

What we can learn from First Aid and needs analysis.

I've been first aid certified since around 2007 and let me tell you the renewal courses can be quite entertaining. Once a seminar lasted about 8 hours or so and at the end of this daunting course we had demonstrate the first air process. One of the attendees got up to demonstrate, and as the attendee began she immediately ran over to the test dummy and started doing chest compressions. The first step in CPR is to assess the scene for hazards, why? Because, the hazard that incapacitated the person on the ground might incapacities you as well or the person might just be sleeping and some random passerby starts doing chest compressions on them.

Like in First Aid, you need to figure out what is going on with the consumer before making snap judgements and proposing solutions. What's going on with the prospect? How long have they been shopping? What's the experience been like so far? When do they want to the policy to start? What prompted them to start now? What do they expect from an agent? Have they had to use their insurance?

Once I had a prospect walk in to talk about a standalone auto insurance policy. He was nice enough to bring his declaration page in with him to the meeting. When he walked in to the office, he was the quintessential California surfer bro. He had ice-tipped spiked hair, sun glasses on backwards, a tommy-b T-shirt, sandals and board shorts that smelled like beach. When he handed me his insurance declaration, it was a limited permissive use, minimum state limits policy with a non-standard insurance carrier. Mind you we only wrote preferred clients as we had no market for non-standard risk at the time. So, I could've made a few choices in this situation, I could have told him he was fine where he was, I could have copied his limits and quoted a minimum policy, and or I could've done what I did. Which was treating him like every single person who walked through my door, the same. I went through my process sales just like I would have with a preferred client. When we started talking I asked him the usual questions. Eventually, we got around to what he did for a living, to which he replied in a somewhat non-descriptive fashion as an artist. What kind of art? Classical art. Interesting, tell me about it? To which he replied, "Well, I restore classical artwork." Ah-ha. Tell me more... To which he replied, "My trust purchases about 10 to 20 million in art work at a time, refinish it and then re-sell it at a mark-up." When he started explaining all of this my business partner, turned around in his chair and you could have placed a ruler in his mouth his jaw dropped so low. I know it's rather cliché to say don't judge a book by its cover, but in our industry you just never know.

Needs Analysis

Theoretically, the liability exposure of a lawsuit is limited to the extent of assets exposed to that lawsuit. So, we need to figure out the extent of assets a client has or intends to accumulate over a lifetime. Since, a judgement can be placed on your income, that theoretical limit can be stretched rather far. What does a client need to protect what they care about most?

Selling the Insurance Company

How do you sell the insurance carrier? Whether you have one option to sell or multiple carriers, you have to sell the value of that company. SO, how do you do that? Sell the time longevity, sell the claims service and sell other factors. What does this insurance company do better than other insurance companies? Why did you select this insurance company? What is the risk placement strategy?

Problem Identification

Why do people talk to insurance agents? People talk to agents because they have a problem or perceived problem and for some reason they think you can solve it. About 75% to 80% of consumers self-reported that price was the driving factor for shopping. So, nearly every person who is shopping thinks price is the problem, right? Maybe the person is overpaying, but if you choose to focus every conversation on price, what happens when you are the not the cheapest guy on the block? A prospect has to agree there is a problem to begin with. Our job is to find it, discuss the problem and then develop buy-in to the solution.

What's the problem?

A client walks into your office complaining about the price, because for the last 5 years it has been going up. What is the problem the insured has? Answer is you don't know yet. The insured then plops down a declaration page of a policy written about 5 years ago on a home with no inflation guard. The Replacement/reconstruction Cost of the home has not be recalculated since the inception of the policy by BLANK insurance carrier. So, what's the problem? The problem is the insured is under-insured, possibly. Let me share an interesting stat with you.

MSB estimates based on that on average

59% of homes/properties are under-insured by at least 22%.

All people care about is price, right? Let me ask you something, if your home burns to the ground are you going to be worried about the price of your insurance? All people care about is price, right? When we shop people care about price, price is always a factor in our decision making processes, but it doesn't have to be the only factor in our process or the sole determinant in our process for purchasing insurance.

What's the Problem?

A loan officer friend of mine sent me a declaration page from a large insurance carrier and asked me to quote it. When reviewing the insurance policy I noticed that there was no auto/home or package discount. Even more alarming I noticed that this policy didn't have an umbrella discount, which this carrier would show on their home declaration page. What's the problem? Most agents would think the problem is that the debt to income ratio is too high for the client and the loan officer wanted to get it down. That is in fact what the loan officer told me.

Owning insurance is the most fundamental responsibility of homeownership, it is **never** where you look to cut costs. If you are looking to cut costs on a $900 insurance policy to get the correct 35% Debt to Income ratio on $500,000+ in debt, then you are not qualified for the home, PERIOD. So, back to my question. What's the problem here? The problem as I saw it, was that the client probably wasn't taking advantage of possible multi-policy discounts. So, I asked the broker if I could reach out to the client. The broker said of course, and that the client has a bunch of other insurance policies as well.

I reached out the client the same day and left a message. The client called me back after speaking with the mortgage officer to confirm who I was. After speaking with the client he told me that he had, a Dp3 (Dwelling Fire Policy) with BLANKER, a standalone umbrella with BLANKUmbrella.com, a home with BLANKCO, an auto with BLANKERS, an earthquake with BLANKOVERA and a motorhome policy with BLANKGRESSIVE. To which, I said, would you mind if I stopped on by and took a look at it. To which the client responded, of course. People care about things they take seriously and things they find important to them. Would it be fair to say that your most valuable assets are of some significance to you? Yeah, no kidding.

The client was paying about $13,000 or so annually, with a perfect and clean loss history. This was the ideal of ideal clients, he had high deductibles and no losses. So, what's the problem? Well, the first problem was that the client had 6 agents and 6 different insurance companies. The other problem was that the client wasn't paying EFT for all those policies and was writing checks every month. I closed this account with a simple question. **Would you consider paying SLIGHTLY more for your insurance if I could put all of your policies with a single company?**

How do I know when I crossed a boundary?

The best way is to verify with a question and then proceed or adapt your line of questioning or in the worst case scenario re-establish rapport. Rapport is a fluid process that involves some uncomfortable tension.

Try these on for starters.

- Lemme ask you John, so far, how does this all sound?
- Lemme ask you something Bob, as a strategy to protect your assets, how does this all sound so far?

Typical Responses

- I think I'd like more information. What does it cost?
- I think it sounds great, let's do this.
- I feel it might be a bit much considering my budget. (Needs more value)
- I feel that could work. (Needs more time)

What we want when selling insurance is to have the client make one important decision based around two questions. What if they remain under-insured and what happens if they spend a little more money to protect their assets?

Selling Insurance on value is rather easy. You ask questions to uncover concerns and problems. Evaluate a prospects current level of protection. Evaluate their assets that might be exposed to loss.

Educate Clients on how insurance works in simple terms if possible with illustrations. Educate clients on their level of exposure, gap in protection and then how your customized solution solves that problem.

But, the key is that you have to get them agree there is a gap and that if they stick with their current insurance plan, it is also a problem. Each person allows for a tolerable level of uncertainty with their risk retention and transfer. Buying insurance is about buying a level of certainty. If I buy collision coverage I am certain in an accident my car will be able to get fixed, assuming it's not a total loss.

Remember, selling insurance isn't about just espousing and enumerating benefits or features. You can rattle off benefits and product knowledge all day long, but the truth is most people don't care. You have to use those questions to get them to care. To help them understand what is at risk and leverage those experiences they may have had in the past.

Selling insurance = What are the Assets Exposed to potential Loss (qualifying by figuring out what people care about), look at the potential causes of loss (educate on how insurance works), and then explain the financial causes of loss (explain how your solution solves the gap or the risk they take by not carrying the proper amount of insurance).

Most people have two options when it comes to personal risk management:

1. **Risk Transfer:** they can buy a 1 million dollar umbrella policy for less than $20 a month.

2. **Risk Retention:** if you have millions of dollars lying around you can pay for legal fees and court costs yourself...

My Sales Strategy for personal P&C.

This is how I developed my selling strategy. Gather the basic underwriting information via phone or email and close with a face to face appointment. How can I maximize the sale? How do I get the client the maximum amount of insurance to fit their specific need for coverage? How is the current insurance lacking or insufficient? What can I offer that is different or unique?

Here is what I came up with:

- Leverage Higher Deductibles.
- Focus on Endorsements.
- Focus on the Right Amount of Insurance.
- Explain the Coverage in Simple Terms.
- Focusing on Protecting Assets with Higher liability limits.
- Focus on a specific clientele.
  - Multiple Auto, No At Fault Accidents, Homeowner/Renter and Umbrella.

Learning to Speak in Future Tense

One thing most new sales people have a hard time doing is planting seeds. When you speak in the future tense you are assuming the close. You're making an assumption that the prospect is going to sign up with you. If we end up working together one thing I want you to think about is... that if you ever get into an accident call me first before you call the insurance company. Sometimes it's in your best interest to not a file claim.

The Exclusive Nature of Insurance

Insurance contracts are very exclusive by nature. Everyone has a customized rate based on their habits and may or may not qualify for certain companies based on their risk. Insurance contracts are not transferable either making them very exclusive.

"What we do is help middle class families protect their assets by ensuring we educate them on their needs and customize the insurance to fit those very specific needs." Or, "If we are able to determine you are the right fit for our Agency and you decide that this is the kind of agency you want protecting your family than..."

Having a good Fact Finding Sheet

How do you gather information? Do you write down the basic info on loose scratch paper? Or do you have an actual comprehensive form? A lot of agents just scratch down enough info to get a quote and kind of guesstimate a lot of details until they can firm up the quote. The quality of your fact finding sheet will tell me a lot about how seriously you take your profession. Ask a lot of questions that will help you not only understand the asset you are trying to insure but the overall risk and the value system of the person you are insuring. Do they care about coverage? Do they think insurance is for maintenance or for the big things?

Educating a client on Personal Property

When educating explain everything in simple terms. Use analogies people can really relate to and easily understand. For instance, how do you explain a personal property limit? One approach is that you can explain how it is a generic percentage of coverage A...

Or...

John, think of your house. Take your house lift it off the ground. Take the roof off and flip it upside down and shake it. Everything that falls out of your house is your personal property. And we cover that property anywhere in the world.

The Art of Pausing

Learning when and how to pause during the sales process is part of the art of selling. Here's how it works. You ask for something, you shut up and wait for a response to the question. There's no exact amount of time to pause, so it takes some practice. During one of my sales presentations for a cold lead, I had made my 'ask' and paused for 3 minutes. This prospect was a cold lead, he came into the office and my offer was significantly higher in both price and coverage. He had a standalone auto policy and I was recommending auto, renters and umbrella insurance. I made my 'ask', handed him the quote and turned slightly away to look at some papers on my desk while he thought it over. I wanted to only turn slightly away to not ignore him but let him know that it was up to him to take it or leave it, I wasn't desperate for the business. I could feel him looking over at me waiting for me to say something. To be honest the papers I was shuffling through were mostly scratch paper. At some point my business partner even turned around in his chair to see what was going on, because you could cut the tension with a knife. He took the proposal and said, "You know what let's do it." That's when I knew I mastered selling. If you can significantly up-sell total strangers, you've mastered selling.

My sales philosophy.

When selling insurance I would operate under a fundamental premise. That premise was most insurance agents did a poor job with field underwriting, most agents didn't sell enough insurance to protect the risk properly or correctly, most agents did not customize the offering or add the appropriate endorsements and most agents didn't bother asking deep questions. These assumptions proved to be for the most part correct and allowed me to sell higher levels of coverage almost in every situation. Which in turn allowed me to maximize the commission of every sale.

Let's say a client brings in a declaration page, what is the first thing you ask yourself? How did they determine this coverage A amount? Most Agents will just focus on the rate and quote to try and beat the rate. But, what I would do and it was a bit different, would be to expose as many errors and weaknesses the other agent made and parlay that to my advantage.

The first thing we did was determine if the coverage A was correct. Most of the time it was too low. Most Agents would not get details on the quality of the bathrooms or kitchens and rate them all standard. We would often find these weaknesses and expose them.

My grandmother has a policy with a very large captive company. Recently she wanted me to review it just to look at it. The Agent who I imagine was purely just thinking about price gave her $450,000 of coverage A on a 2500 SQFT home in Los Angeles... A whopping $165 a SQFT in an area where that home could be worth over $1,500,000! In an area where a proper RC would be around $290/SQFT.

These kind of common errors turn into lawsuits if claims happen. But, to the keen agent they are opportunities to talk about Co-insurance clauses and Demand Surge.

Demand Surge: An easy way to upsell the correct coverage A amount is to explain Demand Surge. Demand surge is simple and this is why we sold so many blanket property policies. Let's say your entire neighborhood burns down to the ground. Your current policy allows for 500,000 of coverage A. Which means they determined the labor, the cost of materials and even profit for the contractor. But, if a bunch of homes suffer from the same fire or whatever type of covered loss then that contractor now will increase the cost of labor and the cost of goods dramatically goes up to meet the new demand for contractors.

The most Common Weakness to exploit in a Home Policy.

- Incorrect Coverage A. (Underinsured home policy)
- No or Low Sewer and Drainage.
- Valuables not endorsed above sub-limits.
- Minimum liability limits on a home policy.
- Minimum Medical Payments on Auto or Home.
- Low Rental limits
- Low UMBI on the Auto.

There is a point in my presentation that I would always call the 'Light-Bulb's-On' moment for the insured. The moment at which you show them their current asset protection and how exposed it is to loss. But, there was right in front of them a customized solution we had that could fix all of that.

The most Common Weaknesses in an Auto Policy

- No Rental Reimbursement

- Rental Car Reimbursement can be the most costly out of pocket expense a person incurs during an accident. A Honda Accord will cost you around $30 per day. For every $1000 in damage it takes about 1 week of repair time.
- Low Rental Car Coverage
- If a client is driving a BMW and has $30/per day limits they are underinsured. It costs $50/per day for a luxury auto in 2017.
- Low Bodily Injury Limits
- Low Under/Uninsured Bodily Injury Limits
- Have low UMBI limits is the stupidest decision a broker/agent can make for their client. Why is that you ask? Because, this is the one coverage that applies to the Insured not the other driver. If the other driver has insufficient limits to pay for the insured medical bills this is the coverage the insured has to rely on.
  - If these coverages are low most law firms will take that into consideration before taking on a client as well.

- Low Medical Payments
  - Again Med Pay is for the Insured passengers and insured. This is coverage to help if the insured is injured.
- Deductible Waiver Missing
  - Parked Car Deductible, Uninsured Motorist Deductible, Hit and run UM Deductible Waiver.
- Low Collision Deductibles.
  - I'll talk more on why this is a bad idea for Collision.

Transitioning

A transition statement or question is simply a way to move from one product to another during the sales process.

Transitioning to Auto

- By the way who is your auto insurance with?
- Well, now that we have covered your home, why don't we look at some options for your auto insurance as well?

- While we put some options together for your home insurance, why don't we take a look at bundling?
- Have you thought about bundling your auto and home?

Transitioning to Home
- John, have you thought about bundling your property/auto?
- By the way who is your renters insurance with?
- Why don't we try to put your renters/auto with the same company?

Transitioning to Umbrella Insurance
- Have you heard of umbrella insurance?
- Would you be interested in lawsuit protection?
- By the way who is your umbrella insurance with?
- What do you think about umbrella insurance?
- I'm curious I don't see protection for major claims on your policy, would you open to talking about umbrella insurance?

But Mike, How do I transition to Umbrella Insurance?

How do you feel about umbrella insurance?

Have you heard of umbrella insurance? Usually, I'd get a response back like, "Yeah it's the one that kind of goes over everything in case of a bad accident, right?" Whatever the answer I would normally just say let me break down for you. If selling insurance is a search for the truth and your clients have any form of assets or plan on having assets the truth is that they need umbrella insurance.

- How much can someone sue you for?
  - Wait for an answer.
  - "I don't think there is a limit." (With a confused look) Or "Millions I imagine."
  - Exactly, for any amount of money. It's unlimited.
- In the State of California, why can someone sue?
  - Wait for an answer.
  - "I... for anything really..."
  - Exactly right. So any reason at all.
  - The reason why I ask about umbrella insurance is that people can sue you for any reason for an unlimited amount of money. Umbrella insurance

will protect your assets from lawsuits up to 1,000,000 or more potentially. (At this point most people are sold)

- Let me ask you something John, "In the State of California if you get into an auto accident what would you guess the average jury award is if your case goes to court?"
  - Wait for an answer.
  - Currently it's around $300,000 per accident and that's the average!
  - Wait for a response.
  - Currently you have $15,000 in protection per accident. If someone ends up suing you because of an accident. Do me a favor subtract $15,000 from $300,000, what does that come out to roughly?
  - Wait for an answer.
  - Exactly, now your deductible went from $500 to $285,000.

- Let me ask you another one, "When someone falls on your property or sues you for any kind of injury what do you think that average jury award is in California?"
  - Wait for an answer.
  - Currently it's around $500,000, conservatively.
  - Wow!
  - (You can repeat the same from above)

But Mike, What if my client says I don't have assets to be sued.

Rebuttal 1: If someone severely injured you in a car crash to the point at which you couldn't work ever again, would you not get a lawyer? If they sue and win they can garnish up to 25% of your wages per pay period.

Rebuttal 2: What do you think it costs to retain an attorney? $25,000 or $30,000? (Most people say, well yeah a good one could be even more than that!) Exactly. With umbrella insurance the insurance company pays the defense cost on top of the jury award. Put the onus on the insurance company to pay the bills not your family.

Rebuttal 3: Remember they can still sue you even if your company determines you to be not at fault for the accident. Imagine paying those defense costs just to prove you're not at fault for the accident.

Transitioning to Life Insurance

The reason I didn't talk a lot of about life insurance in this book is because I wrote an entire book called, "How to Sell Life Insurance." But, for the sake of transitioning to life insurance, it's important to remember that life insurance is an emotional purchase. About 75% of people are prompted to get a quote by an actual agent/person.

The two easiest life transitions I've used as an independent insurance agent were these:

1. (Oh) By the way John, who do you have your life insurance with?

And or

1. Now that we have protected your car or home or business. Why don't we look at your most important assets... your family? John in the event something should happen to you, how do you feel about protecting your family from financial hardship?

   The reason I always used the first transition is simple. It opened up opportunity in a natural way. Because, you get one of three statements that usually always end in an application:

   a. "I have it through work."

And Or

   b. "I don't have life insurance."

And or

   c. "I have a term policy, but I'm not exactly sure how much... I think it's a 100,000, 10 year term."

   If the client would say I have it through

work, then it would allow me to ask some follow up questions. I'd usually start be congratulating them by having something in place. Because, something is better than nothing. But, the opportunity is that it opens up to very important conversations.

d. How much insurance do they need to protect their family?

e. Pretty much every group life insurance policy is one year salary. In the event something should happen to the insured is that enough to protect their family? Odds are it isn't.

f. Do they plan on staying at the job forever?

g. Opens up the discussion for portability and convertibility.

h. With most Group Life Insurance policies you can't take it with you if you leave your job or fired.

i. "It's kind of like renting vs owning a house."

j. That's great! John have you evaluated your insurance needs since you bought the policy?

k. What do you mean?

l. We'll has your life changed over the last 9 years?

m. Of course.

n. Maybe your life insurance needs have to.

o. (Also for number three) That's great! So, how did you arrive at that number?

Ask yourself, as a multi-line agent or broker. Do you even want a client who is completely unwilling to discuss life insurance? Assuming the person doesn't have life insurance, there shouldn't be a lot of pushback to at least setting up a future appointment.

My Sales Philosophy for Commercial P&C.

What matters to a business? The process for Commercial and Personal is more or less the same with different products. There are common important coverages to speak about with a business owner. For instance, did you know what the time deductible is on business income replacement? Most business income replacement has a 3 day time deductible, which means you have to wait until the 4th day until benefits start to kick in. Do you know how to increase the workers compensation limit from 1,000,000 to 10,000,000? The answer is that you can extend commercial umbrella coverage to extend to workers compensation, if done correctly. Do you know what kind of unique risks that industry faces?

Sales Examples

Example #1: P&C 20 year XYZ Insurance Consumer

John walks into your office. He owns a home and has a family.

Agent: John, how long have you had this policy in place? How long have you been with XYZ company?

John: Oh... about 20 years ago or so.

Agent: Well, John let me ask you something, has everything in your life stayed the same over the last twenty years?

John: Of course not. What do you mean?

Agent: Do you think that the value of your home stayed the same over those last 20 years? Gone up? Down? Or stayed about the same?

John: Of course it's gone way up... (Wheels turning

in his head)

Agent: Would you have time to review your coverage this week? What works better for you Tuesday at 10am or Thursday at 10am?

OR ...

Agent: Can I take a look at your current coverage. It looks like your 2000 SQFT home has about $200,000 in coverage, which comes out to $100/SQFT (usually at this point most people realize what that implies). Which at the time this policy was written might have been plenty of coverage (reaffirm they made a good decision when they purchased). I'm pretty familiar with this area and the reconstruction costs. If you were to guess, if your home burned to the ground and you had to rebuild it. What do you think the price per SQFT would be?

John: Definitely not $100/SQFT.

Agent: (Whatever the answer he gives you say, "That's pretty close.") This area for this kind of home would actually be closer $300/SQFT. This part of the conversation usually goes on auto pilot for selling a home policy, even if the premium is higher. This also opens up the conversation to the Demand Surge conversation or Co-Insurance Clauses.

> **Notation from author:** From here what I normally would do is run a MSB calculation with a breakdown of where the money goes in the event of an accident and explain it to the insured.

Example #2: Small Business Owner no EPLI

Example: John is a small business owner who owns let's say an accounting firm or generic small business.

Agent: John, How do you feel about being sued by your employees?

John: I'd rather not if I can avoid it.

Agent: Exactly. And let me ask you why could a disgruntled ex-employee sue you? Or current employee for that matter?

John: Have them list reasons. Or just say any reason.

Agent: Nowadays employers have a big target on

their back. Some people want what you have to put it frankly. EPLI is how we protect everything you've worked so hard for from a disgruntled employee. Whether the employee is making an accurate claim or not they are still going to sue.

John: Can you take a look to see if my current policy covers me?

Example #3: Low Liability Personal Auto

Example: John is a homeowner and has a minimum $100,000 liability on his HO3.

Agent: John I ask every client these two questions.

John: What?

Agent: Let me ask you, why can someone sue you?

John: For any reason. (usually with a little hesitation)

Agent: Exactly right. How much can someone sue you for?

John: There's no limit.

Agent: That's exactly right! People can sue you for any reason for an unlimited amount of money.

Pause. Currently you have 100,000 of coverage on this policy.

Agent: Pause

Agent: Let me ask you one more question John, if you were to guess how large the average liability claim that goes to court, what do you think it would be, roughly?

John: $100,000?

Agent: $450,000 to $1,000,000. The most common claims are dog bites, slip and falls, and injuries to people working on your property.

Example # 4: Low Deductible Client

Example: Client has a $1000 or $500 deductible on a property policy and has not reviewed their insurance in some time or altered it in some time.

Agent: John, can I ask you something?

John: Sure, thing.

Agent: When was the last time you used your insurance? Have you ever had to actually use your insurance?

John: Never. Or it's been about 7 to 10 years.

> **Notation from Author:** Only 1 to 5% of your clients actually use their insurance each year. It takes about 10 years for a client on average to use their home insurance. If this is a preferred client then this answer should be somewhat obvious.

John: Why do you ask?

Agent: Well, I noticed you had a $500 deductible on your home insurance. Can I ask why?

John: Well, that's just what I signed up with.

> **Notation from author:** From here there are multiple talk paths that you can use to increase deductibles. We can sell the concept, we can talk about the savings for having a higher deductible.

Agent: Lemme ask you something John, do you plan on having a claim soon? Do you plan on getting into an accident soon?

John: I sure hope not.

Agent # 1: Well, then why don't we bump up your deductible? If you go another X years without using your insurance then you would save around Y amount per year.

Agent # 2: John, in the event your home would burn to the ground, do you think you could find $5000 to replace it?

Agent # 3: John, how about we get you a better deal and slightly increase that deductible?

Agent # 4: John, if we could get you a better deal by increasing your deductible, would you consider it?

Agent # 5: I'm a little worried about how low your deductible is... pause... have you ever thought about increasing it?

John: $5000! That seems a bit much.

Agent: You're right $5000 is a bit much, let's go with $2500 instead then?

> **Notation from Author:** 95% of our clients had a $2500 home deductible or higher using this simple strategy strategy.

The Trap of Low Deductibles

What is insurance for? Is it for the $100 claims or the $1,000,000 claims? The way I designed my sales presentation was to have that 'ah ha' moment where you are more or less able to take price off the table. Odds are if you file a claim your rates will go up and if the rates go up odds are the client will shop you.

So, how do you prevent this? Proper field underwriting, high deductibles and adding value. Insurance is for the big things. Insurance is not a maintenance policy for your home, it's not meant to be a warranty. People statistically tend to drive safer if they have more to risk, higher deductibles. The premium is more competitive and your loss ratio will be better off as well. This will help you qualify for profit sharing and keep relations solid with your insurance company. Remember if prospects are truly concerned about their budget they will most likely be agreeable with higher deductibles.

But Mike, what about claims the insured is not responsible for?

Let's say you have a theft of $2000 in stolen

patio furniture. Your insured has a $500 deductible. One of my close friends unfortunately had a case just like this. Someone climbed up his retaining wall and stole/tossed down about that much in furniture. They filed a claim and received the $1500 after itemizing the loss for the insurance company. The following renewal had an 83% increase in premium. Worth it? Doubtful.

But Mike, how do I sell a client on higher deductibles?

Here are a few ways:

a. Let me ask you John, when was the last time you were involved in an At-Fault accident? 10 years ago.

b. Let me ask you another question, if your car was totaled in a car crash could you find $1000 to pay for the deductible?

c. If your home burned to the ground do you think $2500 would be reasonable to replace it? Is that something you could do/manage?

These questions do two things. They improve

the price per unit for the amount of insurance your client can purchase and it trains them to think of insurance for the large scale accidents. By implementing this approach you put the small increase in deductible in the scope of what the insurance really gets you. Also, with the lower premium it makes for an easier sale. Trust me the last thing anyone wants to ever do is use their insurance.

But Mike, won't some clients just change their current deductible rather than switching to me?

Yes, of course. Remember this is an odds game and we do everything in our power ethically to increase our odds of closing the sale. Sometimes when we make recommendations people just take them back to their agent. It happens.

"The greatest discovery of my generation is that human beings can alter their lives by altering their attitudes of mind." - William James

Chapter 8: Closing and Objections

In this chapter we are going to tackle the last part of the sales process. We are going to break down Closing and objection handling in specific detail.

Closing

Closing is simple for the most part. Make your 'ask', ask for the sale. Shut up. Wait for an answer. The first person who talks loses. Respond to the answer and negotiate.

Single Product Quote or Account Rounded Approach

If a prospect comes to you for an auto quote, what do you do? Most agents make the mistake of just quoting the auto and moving along. What I hear often is, "Well Mike, I'll sell the auto and then cross-sell on the renewal..." I equate this to the 'Buy term and invest the difference crowd', because yeah in theory we should but no one ever invests the difference. Most agents have little or not cross selling apparatus, but if you think about it you are just creating more work and reducing your chances at retaining the client long-term.

No matter how you attempt to close a sale, it should be done with the affirmative and assumptive methodology in mind.

- How would you like to pay?
- Would you like to get this policy started today or tomorrow?

Most people really drop the ball when it comes to closing a sale. You're asking someone for money. So just ask them for money.

Don't dance around the issue. Just ask and patiently and calmly wait for a response. Remember this is a matter of fact type of conversation you are having with someone. If you have presented correctly, they arrived with you at the conclusion they don't have enough insurance or have the wrong insurance. If they begin to utter something, don't immediately jump in talking about benefits or reminding them why they need something. Just be professional and wait for a response. Digest what they have to say and respond. Have you ever heard the phrase he who talks first loses? This is why.

How do I know when to close a sale?

Before you close you need to know if the customer is ready to be closed. After experience you will know by simply picking up buying signal and the customer will ask buying questions.

Think of a sale like cooking a turkey. You don't shove the turkey into the oven and then turn on the over. It's a front loaded process that requires a lot of preparation. You have to baste the turkey (building rapport), you have to preheat the oven (fact find and qualify) and then you have to cook the turkey (present). And after all that it might come out dry or it might be just right. With some clients you will know when to close based on buying questions and others will take a little more time in the oven so to speak.

Try to build your presentation style around pre-handling objections and getting to truly understand client needs. The best way to do this is by segmenting the customer into those 6 categories we spoke about earlier of shoppers and then by determining if they are think of feel people so we can tailor make our approach to selling.

Presenting Multiple Offers?

Good, Better and Best isn't a good strategy. A great way to never see someone again is by giving them three different quotes with different payment plans and or with different companies... People want guidance, if I wanted to shop for myself and not get expert advice, I wouldn't have called you in the first place.

Remember you are the expert and you came to a conclusion together as to what level of protection will cover their assets and protect their families in the event of a financially devastating accident.

Objections

My Objection Philosophy

When I think about how to handle objections, I think that they should not come up for the most part. Objections are rooted in our own lack of understanding of the prospect. Somewhere along the lien we didn't customize our proposal or presentation to meet the prospects needs or suitability. Really, objections are by in-large a representation of our own process.

Types of Objections

Most Common types of Objections:

- *No Money*: I don't think I can afford that.

- *No Time*: I don't have time right now.

- *No Need*: I'm happy with who I'm with.

- *No trust*: I don't know you.

Objections: Prospecting, Concept, Transitionary & Closing Objections

There are four times during your process when and where a prospect can object. Anytime we get an objection we should inventory it and adjust our process. That being said, the first step is to identify when objections arrive and what they look like.

Prospecting objections

I'm fine with who I'm with.

Concept Objections

That's too much coverage!

I'm just interested in an auto quote.

That's too expensive!

Complaints vs Objections

Sunday night dinners is a big tradition in Italian American households. At Sunday dinner complaining is the centrepiece of the meal. Sometimes people just like to complain. Sometimes when people say, "That's a lot of coverage" What they mean is that is a lot of coverage.

How many objections should I expect during a sales process?

Objections are par for the course. My job when handling objections is to understand the prospects point of view and not try to convince them they are wrong about their objection. Don't be afraid of people saying no. We've become so consumed with the idea of getting the customer to say yes that we cower in fear when they customer says no.

Why do people object?

- We confused the prospect.

- The Prospect is not qualified.

- We didn't answer a question.

- We didn't address a concern.

- Lack of explanation of concepts.

- We talked our self out of a sale

- Lack of certainty

- Lack of trust

- Fell out of rapport

Other Types of Objections

- **Price Objections**
  - That's too expensive!
  - I'm on a fixed budget.

- **Coverage Objections**
  - That's too much coverage!
    - I don't need Earthquake coverage! The deductible is too high!

- **Brokerage/Company/You Objections**
  - I have it through work.
  - My wife's brother's sixth cousin's nephew is my broker.
  - I read a bad review online!
  - I need to talk to my spouse.

The truth is I have read that exact same type of review. Do you think most people write reviews when they have had good experiences or bad experiences? If you look long enough, online you can find a bad review for clean air, puppies and rainbows.

You're right, maybe you should. *Shut up and listen*. If you're relationship with your brother in-law is more important than properly protecting your stuff, I understand. *Look, you lost the sale anyways. Give them time to expand on that.* Maybe they should or maybe it's an excuse they are using to stall.

When I first started selling I was all attitude and no process. I sold purely based on enthusiasm, because I didn't know any better. Who hasn't been a young salesperson? When people told me that they wanted to think about it, at 20 years old I would simply say, "Well John lemme ask you something, What do you have to think about?"

With a decision like this, it makes sense to take some time to think it over to be sure you're getting the best possible value. I'm curious though, what's worrying you the most about the proposal?

What does the person have to think about?

- **The Coverage.**
    - o Do you feel you have enough coverage?
    - o Have you ever actually had to use your insurance?
    - o When was the last time you reviewed your coverage? To make sure it's up to date.
- **The Price.**
    - o Have you ever thought of buying better protection?
    - o Have you ever thought about paying in full for your insurance?
- **The Insurance Company, You & Your Firm.**
    - o How long have you been with Big Captive Co.?

- When was the last time your agent sat down and explained your coverage?
- Why are you shopping? Why now?

Objection: I need to talk to my wife, husband, partner & spouse

This objection only comes up when we are too lazy to ask during our process. Sometimes we aren't even talking to the decision maker. Sometimes people, like myself, consult with their family on financial decisions.

- **Strategy 1**
  - Pre-Handle by Asking.
  - Do you normally consult with anyone when you shop for insurance or are you the one who makes this decision?
- **Strategy 2**
  - Schedule a Follow Up Meeting
- **Strategy 3**
  - Jim, that's a really good idea. Is it fair to say though, that your wife might have some questions? Since I won't be there with you to help answer those questions...

o Do you think she'd have questions about the price, the coverage or the company?

Objection: I don't think I need that much coverage.

Why do people use this objection? For example, let's say you have a 20 year BIG Captive Insurance company customer sitting across the desk from you. These customers generally speaking are very loyal and their insurance is generally under-insured. The trick I see most used from these agents is under-insuring the property and using extended replacement cost to make the difference. So, the ITV (Insure to Value) is around 80% of where it should be. So, not only is the property under-insured but the premium is going to be lower than a properly insured policy.

The Goal: Make the conversation about the Reconstruction Cost and value.

Think people: Approach it from a numbers standpoint. Explain the Replacement cost calculator, explain how we calculate it and what it's made up of. Would you consider paying slightly more for your insurance if I could get you better coverage?

Feel people: For feel people I used to use a paused approach. "I'm... a little worried... about your level of protection... Do you feel that you have the right amount of coverage? Do you feel that you have enough coverage if your home burned to the ground?" When was the last time your agent sat down to review you had up to date coverage? Do you think your home has increased in value over the last twenty years?

"Education survives when what has been learnt has been forgotten." - B.F. Skinner

Chapter 9: Cross-Selling and Up-Selling

Cross-selling and Up-selling is life blood of an insurance agency. Our entire industry is predicated on a simple promise, a promise that is wrapped in a nice warm blanket of trust. Insurance is a lot like an airbag, because it requires a lot of trust. It's one of those things you never use, until you have to use it. If you are unfortunate enough to actually have to use it you trust that the insurance company will pay the claim. If a consumer has policies scattered around with multi-carriers and multiple agencies, do you trust they will stick around? Do you trust the other agents will be too lazy to cross-sell? If we are going to maximize every sale, we need to both cross-sell and up-sell every single account.

Cross Selling

Why should we cross-sell?

Did you know that Amazon.com makes 35% of it's revenue from cross-selling? Ever wonder why you see the 'Others who purchased BLANK also purchased BLANK'? Because, it's generating billions of dollars by just subtly suggesting cross-selling. Cross-selling will help you maximize each sale, lower the amount of follow-up work per account and increase retention by proxy of high PIF/Density.

Did you know that 75% of clients will only purchase what you sold them at the first point of sale? Think about it from the prospective of the client. If you didn't sell me the product before, then why do I need it now? Here are some easy ideas.

What can an agent cross-sell?

- Earthquake Insurance
- Flood Insurance
- Umbrella
- Life Insurance
- Auto/ No Home
- Home/ No Auto
- Personal Article Floaters

Prospect Your Book of Business

Start by creating a few lists of current clients or past clients:

1. Auto/No Home
2. Home/No Life
3. Auto/Home/No Life
4. Auto/Home/No Umbrella

Also, if you are looking for life insurance opportunities create lists of clients. For instance, clients turning 55+, clients with expiring term policies, clients who have X-dates within 90 days.

It's important to reach clients about 90 days prior to the renewal as that is generally when the rate increase indications come out.

Another great way to prospect your book of business for life opportunities is looking at clients with recent claims. Someone once said, "Never let a good crisis go to waste."

Do you want fries with that? Cross Selling

If you are struggling to sell concepts the first way to get your sales numbers up is by just asking. If you are new to selling insurance and don't have the slick statements, personal examples, client stories and or questions you are comfortable using, start by using the Mcdonald's method. Just start by learning to ask. A lot of selling is knowing when to ask and when not to ask, how to ask and how not to ask, who to ask and whom not to ask a certain question.

Why should we Up-sell?

Do you know the easiest way to double your rate of growth? All you have to do is make a habit of adding these endorsements onto a home policy for each client over a 5 year period on an umbrella, maximum water back-up sewer and drainage endorsement, max extended replacement cost, a PAF for a wedding ring and personal injury.

Where can an agent find Up-Sell opportunities? YOUR CURRENT BOOK OF BUSINESS!!!!!!!

What can an agent up-sell?

- Higher Deductibles
- Higher Limits of Liability
- Extended Replacement Cost
- Personal Injury
- Rental Car Coverage
- Towing
- Collision Deductible Waiver
- Uninsured Motorist Bodily Injury
- Higher Replacement Cost on Home

What are easy ways to up sell?

Here are some lists that might help you get those creative marketing ideas going:

1. Clients with 100/300/50.
2. Clients with low or no sewer and drainage.
3. Clients with no Home Ins Inflation Rider.
4. Clients with no PAF.
5. Auto No Medical Payments (Quick note on Med Payments, it's the most important and undersold part of an Auto Policy)
6. Clients with Low UMBI.
7. Clients with no collision and no UMPD.
8. Collision no deductible waiver.
9. Collision no rental or low rental.
10. Clients with low deductibles.
11. Clients with no glass buy back deductible.

Index of Questions

- How long have you been with Big Captive Insurance?
- John I noticed that you didn't have Water Back-Up Sewer and Drainage endorsed on your home insurance, can I ask why?
- Is this something you want coverage for?
- What do you do for a living/fun?
- How long have you been doing that for?
- What do you like about it?
- How did you get into that? (Job or Activity)
- What do you do really well?
- When would be a good time to come by the office? Or would you rather meet at your home or business?
- Would you be able to meet on Tuesday at 6 or Thursday at 6? Which time would work better for you?
- Now what's a good time of day to meet morning, afternoon or evening?
- Okay, besides price what do you care about?

- Well, let me ask you something Bob, if I could find a way to bundle all of your policies, would that be something you would consider paying a little more for that?
- What brings you by today?
- Okay, why do you feel that way? (Or better yet) When was the last time your Agent reviewed your coverage?
- Is this a good time to talk?
- Think you'd have 1 minute to talk?
- Is this a bad time to talk?
- Are you too busy to talk?
- Before we get started tell me, what kind of questions or concerns do you have about your current insurance?
- How can I help?
- What brings you by today?
- How do you feel about your current insurance protection?
- What else besides blank are you concerned about?
- Do you feel you have enough insurance?
- How do you feel about Sewer Back Up Coverage?

- How do you feel about insuring your wife's wedding ring? I noticed that you didn't have BLANK on your policy, can I ask why?
- Would you consider paying slightly more for your insurance if I could put all your policies in one spot? Or get you better coverage?
- Besides price, what's important to you?
- How much does an ambulance ride cost? Will your health insurance cover it?
- How much does a retainer on a good attorney cost?
- What do you like about your current plan?
- What are you looking to do?
- Lemme ask you John, so far, how does this all sound?
- Lemme ask you something Bob, as a strategy to protect your assets, how does this all sound so far?
- How do you feel about umbrella insurance? Have you heard of umbrella insurance?
- When someone falls on your property or sues you for any kind of injury what do you think that average jury award is in California?

- "In the State of California if you get into an auto accident what would you guess the average jury award is if your case goes to court?
- If someone severely injured you in a car crash to the point at which you couldn't work ever again, would you not get a lawyer?
- (Oh) By the way John, who do you have your life insurance with?
- Now that we have protected your car or home or business. Why don't we look at your most important assets... your family? John in the event something should happen to you, how do you feel about protecting your family from financial hardship?
- John, how long have you had this policy? How long have you been with XYZ company?
- Well, John let me ask you something. Has everything in your life stayed the same over the last twenty years?
- Has the value of your home stayed the same over those last 20 years?

- Would you have time to review your coverage this week? What works better for you Tuesday at 10am or Thursday at 10am?
- What do you think the price per SQFT would be?
- John How do you feel about being sued by your employees?
- And let me ask you why could a disgruntled ex-employee sue you? Or current employee for that matter?
- How much can someone sue you for?
- Why can someone sue you?
- Let me ask you one more question John, if you were to guess how large the average liability claim that goes to court, what do you think it would be, roughly?
- When was the last time you used your insurance? Have you ever had to actually use your insurance?
- Well, I noticed you had a $500 deductible on your home insurance. Can I ask why?
- Lemme ask you something John, do you plan on having a claim soon? Do you plan on getting into an accident soon?

- Well, then why don't we bump up your deductible?
- John, in the event your home would burn to the ground, do you think you could find $5000 to replace it?
- John, how about we get you a better deal and slightly increase that deductible?
- I'm a little worried about how low your deductible is... pause... have you ever thought about increasing it?
- You're right $5000 is a bit much, let's go with $2500 instead then?
- Let me ask you John, when was the last time you were involved in an At-Fault accident? 10 years ago.
- Let me ask you another question, if your car was totaled in a car crash could you find $1000 to pay for the deductible?
- If your home burned to the ground do you think $2500 would be reasonable to replace it? Is that something you could do/manage?
- How would you like to pay?
- Would you like to get this policy started today or tomorrow?

Other Insurance Sales Books

2. How to Sell Life Insurance.: Life Insurance Selling Techniques, Tips and Strategies Jan 27, 2018

3. How to Sell Indexed Universal Life Insurance: Using a Supplemental Life Insurance Retirement Plan. Feb 19, 2018

4. How to Sell Property and Casualty Insurance.: Understanding Insurance Sales, Tips and Techniques. Feb 3, 2018

5. How to Sell Indexed Universal Life Insurance. : Using a Supplemental Life Insurance Retirement Plan. Second Edition Dec 8, 2018

6. How to Sell Annuities: Annuity Sales Techniques, Tips and Strategies. Mar 12, 2018

7. How to Start and Build an Insurance Agency. Edition 2: An Insurance Agency and Brokerage Guidebook. Jul 30, 2018

8. How to sell Annuities. Second Edition: Annuity Sales Techniques, Tips and Strategies. Jan 13, 2019

9. The Great American Protection Crisis of 2034: Pension Maximization Using an Indexed Universal Life Policy May 31, 2018

10. How to Sell Auto and Home Insurance: A guide to Qualifying and Presenting. Mar 25, 2018

11. How to Start and Build an Insurance Agency. Edition 2: An Insurance Agency and Brokerage Guidebook. Jul 31, 2018

12. "I only smoke when I drink...": Easy ways to have hard conversations as a life agent. Jan 2, 2019

13. How to Sell Indexed Universal Life Insurance.: Using a Supplemental Life Insurance Retirement Plan. Second Edition Dec 9, 2018

14. How to Sell Umbrella Insurance 2nd Edition: A guide to qualify, present and close. Jan 15, 2019

15. How to Sell Umbrella Insurance.: A guide to Qualify, Present and Close. Mar 18, 2018

16. How to Market a Modern Insurance Agency.: New School and Old School Marketing Systems. Apr 29, 2018

17. How to Sell Auto and Home Insurance. Second Edition: A guide to qualifying, presenting and closing. Jan 26, 2019

18. Insurance Agency Economics: An Insurance Agent's guide to Insurance Agency Economics._Feb 4, 2019

Summation

There is not bad investment in education. Selling insurance is unlike any other type of sales profession in the world. You are selling someone a promise. You don't hand them something after the sale, something tangible. You enter an agreement that no one in the agreement ever wants to actualize. The insurance company doesn't want you to use your insurance, the agent doesn't want you to use it and heaven forbid the customer does, because that means they suffered some kind of loss. This is what has made the industry so focused on price and shifting towards comoditzation and direct writers. If you took the time to read this book, or even part of this book, that tells me you care. You care enough about retaining the vestiges of our profession and adding value to your practice. Insurance agents didn't exist at the early stages of our industry and may not in the future, who knows. Thanks for taking the time to read my book and there are many others that you might find valuable in your pursuit.

Sales Rules

Rule Number 1: Don't Complicate Something Simple.

Rule number one of selling insurance is to keep it simple and to the point. We are selling insurance not building a space ship. Most consumers don't know what they don't know. Most consumers don't know what they have, what they need, what they're current risk profile looks like and what they are missing out on. Explain the concepts in digestible terms that consumers can actually understand and stray away from using too much insurance jargon.

About 5 years ago or so, I had the misfortune of sitting through a long-winded sales consultation with a life agent appointed by one of the world's largest life insurance companies. The life agent had a well thought out, but thoroughly confusing Indexed Universal Life Presentation. After about 45 minutes of this rep carrying on I started wondering if she actually was going to stop talking and listen.

Rule Number 2: Always be agreeable.

Selling is as much an art as it is a science. There is no formula for agreeableness, some people are naturally more agreeable than others. Just know that the more confrontational we are as salespeople the worse your odds are for closing a sale. The first person to agree is generally the one that is going to have the advantage during the negotiating process. When we agree we are changing the language of the typical sales process, in that, this is not going to be an 'I'm right and you're wrong' type of conversation. This conversation is going to be a collaborative experience.

Rule Number 3: Understand the Person.

Don't make snap judgements about what someone can afford. Dig. Take the time to ask questions and understand the person sitting across the table. One day a 'surfer dude' walked into my office, dressed in shorts, a Tommy B shirt, shades on the back of his head, tattered sandals and enough wrist bands to make Johnny Depp envious. What was he looking for? This surfer dude was looking for auto insurance and brought in his Dec page. Now, what would most people assume at this point? Well, clearly he is a candidate for 15/30 state minimum limits, right? Wrong! Turns out his current Dec page did have 15/30, but I started digging the same way I would have for an advanced markets case.

Turns out this surfer dude, who did in fact surf, was also in need of some better insurance. Great, do you own or rent? Currently, he was renting an apartment. So, tell me about the apartment, to which he replied, it's all right. Okay, what do you do for a living? To which he replied, 'I'm an artist.' When I started digging a little further into what that meant, it turns out to my surprise that this gentleman restored art in the ball park of $7,000,000 to $15,000,000 pieces of classical artwork. All of which he kept in his home. Now, how does a person like this get 15/30? According to the prospect, turned client, no one ever bothered to have the conversation with him. Everyone assumed he needed state minimums because his current Dec page had state minimums.

Rule Number 4: The Prospect Needs to understand you.

Ask yourself does the prospect have enough information to know, like and trust me? According to Bob Berg all things being equal this is the determining ethos people use for selecting whom to do business with. If not, then you need to build that trust through conversation. Why should this person do business with and not the other guy down the street?

Rule Number 5: Reciprocity

If an insurance sale is a search for the truth we need to follow the rule of reciprocity. The rule of reciprocity makes the insurance buying process a collaborative effort not a confrontational one. Follow a simple rule of thumb, give before you get.

Remember you make no money until the person signs up with you, so you are educating them for free. This is the key to reciprocity. You ask questions to evoke emotions during the process and client has questions that you answer to provide certainty.

Rule Number 6: Stick to a process.

One of my friends had something in her eye and she kept rubbing it to no avail. I passed onto her a simple process I learned, 'close your eye and drag your find down the top and up the bottom halves of your lids, like a windshield wiper.' It's a process that I learned and actually works rather well. To which she replied, 'you have a process for everything.' That didn't used to be the case, I used to be the sales guy who was all personality and energy. This is an overrated sales style that most novice salespeople cling to.

Every person is different, but every sale is exactly the same. In that, people give you the same responses, the same objections and will follow a path. When you start selling insurance it's important to remember that you have a start, you build rapport, you ask questions that are open ended, you find a problem if one exists, and you build a solution/close.

Tension Threshold Principle

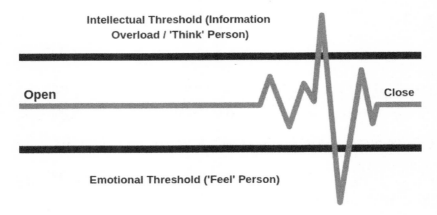

There are two types of people that sit in front of you. There are think type of people and feel type of people. What I mean is that people respond to questions in different ways. Some people say, "I think..." and some people say, "I feel..."

The reason why you need to grasp this concept, is the fact that during a sale we have these invisible boundaries. Emotional or feel people require stories and think people require figures and facts. Not everyone is the same. But, there is a limit for feel people and there is a limit for think people that we have to monitor in the sales process.

Some prospects believe it or not just enjoy talking to sales people and have no intention of buying. Being a salesperson you must think that is somewhat crazy, I did. But, it's true. During your presentation it's important to know when people are giving off buying signals and asking buying questions. Why? Because, that will give you a strong indication of when someone is ready to be closed.

Think of a sale like a Turkey in the oven. First you have to marinate the turkey. Then you preheat the oven. After your prep work is complete and the oven is at the right temperature you put the Turkey in the oven. Some turkeys require more prep work because some are FROZEN and some are fresh. You cook the turkey and check the temperature along the way. But, you have to keep marinating the turkey as it cooks. If the internal temperature is correct after X amount of hours you pull it out and it's moist. If you leave it in too long it dries out or maybe even burns or becomes ruined.

I'll make an effort to dispense with the food

analogies for the rest of the book. Think of it this way. Think of it like an index. The 'Closability' index. Some people are easier to close than others and some require a tremendous amount of effort. But, either way the prospect will ask buying questions.

Well, what's a buying question? For instance, "How much does this cost?" If you are not interested in a product you do not ask how much it will cost. Simple.

Rule Number 8: Ask Open Ended Questions

If you are new to sales or new to insurance. Your best friend is the ability to ask open ended questions and leading questions. Would you mind if we talked about open ended questions? This is a directive question asking for permission to ask a question. How do you feel about annuity sales? What do you think about annuity sales? Whatever the answer always remember to ask follow up questions. You have two ears and one mouth so as a ratio ask too questions before you start to babble on about insurance.

Rule number 9: Set Expectations

Like in any relationship you need to set boundaries. What should a client come to expect of you? What do you expect of a client? A lot of Agents (including myself) tell a client that they meet with each client once per year to make sure the insurance is current or on target. There is nothing customized about that statement for a client. Instead why not just ask. How often would you like to meet each year to discuss your insurance? Most of my clients find once a year to meet their needs but some prefer a call once a quarter to check in.

Rule Number 10: Don't lose control of the conversation.

Probably the most common challenge for newer agents is not maintaining focus. A prospect is going to focus on price if you let them and it can derail the conversation. Price is merely the cost of value. It's your job to educate and present the value. Remember you are the expert and what you focus on will direct the conversation. Don't avoid talking about price, but at the same time don't rush or lead with price. See Diagram Below.

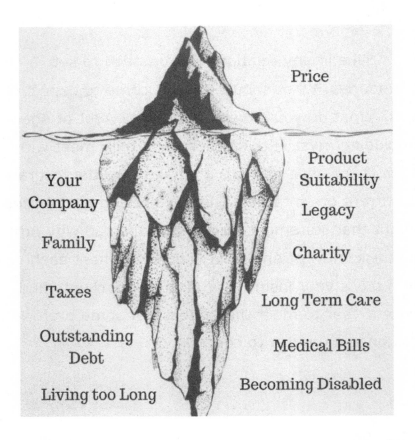

Price

Product Suitability

Legacy

Your Company

Charity

Family

Long Term Care

Taxes

Medical Bills

Outstanding Debt

Becoming Disabled

Living too Long

Rule Number 11: Don't always try to reinvent the wheel.

My father was a carpenter and used to say the nail that sticks out tends to get hammered. Craft your approach as you learn your trade. If your trade is selling insurance, then read, apply and learn. It's important as you craft your style/approach to make adjustments. Somethings might work and somethings might not. But, start by learning from others and adopting an approach and then putting your unique spin on it.

For some people the grass is always greener on the other side of the fence. There are proven systems and sales techniques that you can copy, adopt and emulate. When I first started selling insurance I fell prey to the 'my-way-is-always-better' syndrome, I like to call it learning the hard way.

Rule Number 12: Speak in Future Tense

Learn to speak in the future tense. As your Agent... fill in the blank statement. While I was going to college I paid my way by being a Personal Trainer. I learned very quickly to speak in the assumptive future tense. As your blank... here's how I can be of service to you. "Well, I haven't said I would sign up with you yet." This is the response I want to hear from a client, a soft objection or they might ask buying questions and be able to be closed on the spot. I'm planting seeds not seeds of doubt. But, planting a picture in their head to so some thinking. Picturing in their head how working with me is going to look like and benefit them.

Rule Number 13: Ask for Permission to Ask for the Sale

This is by far my favorite rule and the most overlooked by most insurance salespeople. Along time ago my great grandfather taught me, 'to never open a man's (families) refrigerator without asking for permission.' Why? Because, it's rude among other reasons that might not be as culturally relevant in today's society. When selling make sure to ask for permission to ask for the sale. What I mean is that prior to presenting make sure to ask if it's okay to present a solution. Put some curiosity in there, check the rapport and ask for permission. Don't force your sales pitch on someone.

Rule Number 14: Don't Present Price Present a Solution.

New salespeople present themselves, because they don't know any better other than to be eager, overzealous, and enthusiastic. Transactional salespeople present on price and only price as the focus. Relationship based salespeople present a product that comes with them as the center piece of value. Consultative sales people present a product and focus on coverage needs. The best salespeople present a solution to a problem and the insurance is vehicle to fulfill the problem/solution dynamic.

Rule Number 15: Put yourself in a position to win.

Often we try to sell anyone who can fog a mirror. It happens. The hardest lesson to learn as an agent is that not everyone is a customer. People who walk into your office might not be qualified to buy what you are offering. Don't put yourself into a position to fail by trying to qualify and sell everyone. Remember learning about the gold rush? Prospectors sat in rivers sifting through dirt, swirling water in a dish to find flakes of gold. What they were not trying to do was turn that dirt into gold.

Rule Number 16: Dance through the pain

Persistency is the number one indicator of longevity for a salesperson. Roughly, 97% of life insurance agents and financial advisors fail in the first year. Why? Persistency. We get constantly rejected, again and again. It's not easy to bounce back up and will yourself to keep going.

Rule Number 17: Have a Personal Story

Having a personal story can make or break your sales presentation. If you don't have a compelling reason for doing what you do, sales becomes infinitely more challenging. After witnessing the 'great recession' I had family members lose 50% of their 401k's and qualified plans, almost overnight. What would have happened if they took immediate annuities on their 401k's? They wouldn't have lost a dime. Now granted a lot of that value was regained, but it took 10 years! Imagine waiting to liquidate your life savings for ten years into your retirement.

Made in United States
Orlando, FL
28 January 2022

14175322R00114